THE STUDENT GUIDE TO SUCCESSFUL ONLINE LEARNING

A Handbook of Tips, Strategies, and Techniques

KEN W. WHITE

*Everett Community College and
University of Phoenix Online Campus*

JASON D. BAKER

Regent University

Boston   New York   San Francisco
Mexico City   Montreal   Toronto   London   Madrid   Munich   Paris
Hong Kong   Singapore   Tokyo   Cape Town   Sydney

Executive Editor and Publisher: *Stephen D. Dragin*
Senior Editorial Assistant: *Barbara Strickland*
Senior Editorial-Production Administrator: *Beth Houston*
Editorial-Production Service: *Walsh & Associates, Inc.*
Marketing Manager: *Tara Whorf*
Composition and Prepress Buyer: *Linda Cox*
Manufacturing Buyer: *Andrew Turso*
Cover Administrator: *Joel Gendron*
Electronic Composition: *Publishers' Design and Production Services, Inc.*

Between the time Website information is gathered and then published, it is not unusual for some sites to have closed. Also, the transcription of URLs can result in typographical errors. The publisher would appreciate notification where these errors occur so that they may be corrected in subsequent editions.

Library of Congress Cataloging-in-Publication Data

The student guide to successful online learning : a handbook of tips, strategies, and
  techniques / Ken W. White, Jason D. Baker, editors.
     p. cm.
  Includes bibliographical references and index.
  ISBN 0-205-34104-7
  1. Distance education—Computer-assisted instruction—Handbooks, manuals,
etc. 2. Education, Higher—Computer-assisted instruction—Handbooks,
manuals, etc. 3. Internet in higher education—Handbooks, manuals, etc.
I. White, Ken, W. II. Baker, Jason D.

LC5803.C65S78 2003
371.3'58—dc22   2003053677

Printed in the United States of America

10 9 8 7 6 5 4 3 2 1   07 06 05 04 03

CONTENTS

CHAPTER 3

Selecting an Online Program   21

James Holst

CHAPTER 4

A Taxonomy of Online Courses   33

Jason D. Baker

CHAPTER 5

Communicating in the Online Classroom   43

Ken W. White

CHAPTER 6

Touring the Online Classroom   55

Cliff Lines and Doris E. Sweeney

CHAPTER 7

Know Thyself: Taking Charge of Your Online Learning 65

Margaret Martinez

CHAPTER 8

The Online Instructor's Point of View 79

Judy Donovan

CHAPTER 9

Tips for Online Reading, Writing, and Discussion   89

Carolyn Gale

CHAPTER 10

Learning Communities in Online Classrooms   99

Holly McCracken

CHAPTER 11

Working in Online Groups   111

Deana L. Molinari

CHAPTER 12

Dealing with Online Conflict   123

Ken W. White

CHAPTER 13

Connecting for Success in the Online Classroom   137

Robert H. Woods, Jr. and Samuel Ebersole

CHAPTER 14

Online Mathematics Courses   151

Jeffrey Crabill

CHAPTER 15

Studying in the Online Library   161

Rita Barsun

CHAPTER 16

I Have My Online Degree—Now What Do I Do?   169

Leslie Bowman

Epilogue   185

Ken W. White, Tina Marie Nies, and Jason D. Baker

Index   195

PREFACE

The Student Guide to Successful Online Learning has three central aims. The first is to help students understand the phenomenon of online education: to describe its essential components, to provide examples of how it works, and to set out an experiential base for this activity. The second aim is to examine the various methods, techniques, and approaches that can be used by students seeking to be more effective and successful online learners. To this end, this book provides various "case studies" of successful online practices, and offers specific exercises designed to foster online student success and satisfaction. The third aim is to explore the opportunities for students to become actively engaged in creating their own online learning experience. In short, we take the reality of online education seriously, and want students to take responsibility for making their own choices and for reflecting on alternative ways of thinking and acting in the online world.

The book offers novice online students a highly effective introduction, and serves as a highly useful reference source for those more experienced in online learning. It emphasizes a "self-directed" approach to successful online learning, and tools for the online student to employ in participating in more effective online learning experiences. Among the most significant of these strategies is effective online communication to maximize participation and learning in the online environment.

Chapters focus on selecting an online program; types of online courses; communication in the online classroom; taking charge of your online learning; the online instructor's point of view; tips for online reading, writing, and discussing; online learning communities; online group work; dealing with online conflict; online mathematics courses; using the online library; and what to do after you get your online degree.

Whether online education is in your immediate plans or not, this practical handbook will provide nuggets of insight into an increasingly significant instructional delivery method and learning opportunity.

SPECIAL FEATURES OF THIS BOOK

Certain features distinguish this book from other works about successful online learning. Following are the most significant of these features.

Chapter Length

Shorter chapters allow you to spend less time reading and underlining, and more time reflecting on your own behavior in the online classroom. As an online student, you are accepting the responsibilities that come along with online learning. As a more conscientious learner, you gain additional benefit from the brevity of the chapters. You will easily be able to read each chapter more than once and give yourself the opportunity to master the material and skills better.

Chapter Objectives

Each chapter is introduced by learning objectives that offer specific outcomes that the chapter will demonstrate. These objectives not only serve to preview ideas, but they show a common understanding on the part of the contributors that the quality of learning depends on what online students can *do*, not only on what they *know*.

Application Exercises

Each chapter is followed by an application exercise or two that asks you to apply the ideas of the chapter to your own situation. These application exercises not only serve to review ideas, but they give you an important opportunity to reflect on your own online learning.

"Email" Preferred to "E-Mail"

What is the correct spelling of "email?" Is it "e-mail?" APA styling hasn't directly touched this one yet, though the fifth edition of the *Publication Manual of the American Psychological Association* uses "e-mail." Although some dictionaries advocate "e-mail" because it's analogous to other initialized words (*T-shirt* for example), no one rule has been established for this abbreviation. You'll see that the search engine *Lycos* uses "email." *Microsoft Word* spellchecker suggests both forms. Literate people use both "email" and "e-mail." We prefer "email" to "e-mail," as we prefer "online" to "on-line."

ACKNOWLEDGMENTS

Ken is grateful for his two sons, Nathan and Jamie, for being constant reminders of the importance of always learning. He is also grateful for Holly Clise, for her loving support and friendship, and for her precise and intelligent copyediting of the manuscript. He thanks Robert Allen, Klaus Brandl, Steve Burr, Terry Chadsey, Ken Lysen, Paul Marshall, and Gary Vallat for their friendship; and the University of Phoenix Online Campus for the continuing opportunity to learn the ideas in this book. He also thanks his co-editor, Jason Baker, for joining this project at a challenging time in Ken's life. Jason supplied the initial energy to get this book off the ground, and exemplified the power of authentic collaboration.

Jason would like to thank Ken White for his willingness to bring aboard a co-editor whom he never met face to face. It was a fruitful collaboration but one that would have never occurred without Ken's confidence and trust. He would also like to thank Alan Arroyo, Dean of Regent University's School of Education, for his encouragement and support throughout this project. Most of all, Jason thanks his wife, Julianne, for walking him step by step through this journey, and to Connor and Caleb for their patience while Dad worked on the manuscript.

We would appreciate hearing your comments regarding this handbook. You can email us at:

Ken W. White   *white_kenw@msn.com*
Jason D. Baker   *jasobak@regent.edu*

ABOUT THE AUTHORS
AND CONTRIBUTORS

AUTHORS

Ken W. White holds an M.Ed., an M.A., and a Ph.D. in Speech Communications from the University of Washington. He is a faculty member at Everett Community College in Washington State, where he teaches education and speech classes, and is a recipient of "The Outstanding Faculty of the Year" award from the associated students of Everett Community College. He specializes in organizational, interpersonal, and instructional communication, and once assisted the College of Arts and Sciences at the University of Washington to develop and initiate a nationally recognized training program to improve the performance of undergraduate faculty and teaching assistants. Ken has written a number of journal articles and books, including *Organizational Communication: An Introduction to Communication and Human Relation Strategies* (Simon and Schuster Custom Publishing), and *The Online Teaching Guide* (Allyn and Bacon). He has taught online courses for the University of Phoenix (UOP) for ten years in the areas of general education, organizational communication and behavior, and ethics. He served as Assistant Department Chair for General Studies at the UOP Online Campus, San Francisco, and is a past member of the university's Academic Cabinet. He can be contacted at *white_kenw@msn.com*.

Jason D. Baker is an associate professor of education at Regent University, where he teaches and conducts research about online distance education. He earned a Ph.D. in Communication, an M.A. in Education, and B.S. in Electrical Engineering. Prior to his position at Regent, he worked as an educational consultant at Loyola College in Maryland. Jason has written a number of Internet-related books and articles for academic and popular audiences. He has advised and trained faculty in the use of educational technology, both in traditional classes and in the design of online classes, and has been an active online instructor and distance learner since 1996. In his spare time, Jason advises prospective distance learners about nontraditional Christian education programs through his Web site at *http://www.bakersguide.com*. He can be reached via email at *jasobak@regent.edu*.

CONTRIBUTORS

Wallis C. Metts, Jr. is chair of the Communication Department at Spring Arbor University, where he teaches courses in journalism, communication theory, and media literacy. He piloted an online course for the college in the summer of 1998 and has been teaching online and technology-enhanced courses ever since. He has written articles for over 60 magazines and newspapers and has won national awards for writing and editing for children and teens. He has a Ph.D. in Interdisciplinary Studies (communication, English, and religious studies) from Michigan State University. Dr. Metts can be reached online at *http://www.arbor.edu/~wmetts* or *wmetts@arbor.edu*.

James Holst has over six years of experience as both a student and a facilitator in online education. He earned an M.B.A. in Technology Management from the University of Phoenix Online and B.S. in Natural Science from Lyndon State College. Jim also acts as an online facilitator for the University of Phoenix where his duties include curriculum development, faculty training, and course facilitation in technology and business classes. Besides teaching, Jim works in customer service management and is also an officer in the United States Naval Reserve. Jim lives in New Hampshire with his wife and daughter and can be reached at *james_holst@yahoo.com*.

Cliff Lines is a career naval officer with more than twenty years in the U.S. Navy. He has a master's degree in Educational Technology from George Washington University and is pursuing a doctorate in Distance Learning from Regent University in preparation for a second career in Education. Cliff lives in Norfolk, Virginia, with his wife, Teresa, and two children, Stacy and Christopher. Cliff can be reached online at *cliff-lines@cox.net*.

Doris E. Sweeney, Ph.D., is a 25-year-plus K-12 career educator in regular and exceptional education. She has also taught both undergraduate and graduate levels in traditional/face-to-face and online teacher education program formats. She is married, the mother of two grown children, and writes poetry in her "free" time. Doris can be contacted online at *dsweeney@waldenu. edu*.

Margaret Martinez, CEO at the Training Place, has worked in the fields of learning, information, and technology for more than fifteen years. Previously she was the Worldwide Training and Certification Director for WordPerfect Corporation. Maggie's professional initiatives have focused on demystifying the world of learning and performance by pioneering individual learning difference and personalization research. This research highlights the powerful impact of emotions and intentions on learning and performance. She has a Ph.D. in Instructional Psychology and Technology, regularly presents at major conferences, and publishes in academic and trade publications. She can be contacted online at *www.trainingplace.com* or *mmartinez@trainingplace.com.*

Judy Donovan has been a distance educator with a variety of institutions since the mid-nineties. She teaches high school, undergraduate, and graduate classes through a variety of platforms—online and face-to-face—in many different subjects. She is particularly interested in convincing preservice teachers that technology is an exciting area for teaching and learning. Judy recently completed her Ed.D. in Instructional Technology and Distance Education and can be contacted at *http://www.jkdonovan.com* or *jkdonovan@aol.com.*

Carolyn Gale is the program director of Stanford University's Research Communication Program. She has five years experience designing and evaluating online courses and workshops for university engineering and management programs. She holds a B.S. in Computer Science and an M.S. in Instructional Technology, both from Vanderbilt University. She can be reached online at *http://www.stanford.edu/~cgale/* or *cgale@stanford.edu.*

Holly McCracken has been involved in teaching and developing instructional curricula for 27 years in the areas of land-based, media-based, and Web-based instruction. She is currently employed as the director of Distance Education for the College of Liberal Arts and Sciences at the University of Illinois at Springfield (UIS). Additionally, she is an instructor at UIS in the Applied Studies, Liberal Studies, and Credit for Prior Learning Programs. She also works at Capella University in the Training and Performance Improvement, Instructional Design, and Online Teaching and Training Programs, and is a trainer with the Illinois Online Network, at the University of Illinois Online. Her professional specializations include adult education, instructional design, program development and administration, and media-based instructional delivery. You can contact Holly via email at *hollymac@royell.net.*

Deana L. Molinari is finishing her dissertation in instructional psychology and technology. She has worked as a nurse, educator, and entrepreneur. Her research interests are in health promotion and online education. Her completed research studies include a qualitative study of the microfunctions of online communication; an action research study of online facilitation of problem solving groups; comparisons of microcommunication functions; patterns and transitions of worst and best outcome groups; validation in online groups; comparison of online and face-to-face collaborative groups; the social support needs of families adopting special needs children; critical thinking and learning orientation of beginning nursing students; and the learning orientation and healthy practices of seniors. She can be reached online at *dmolinari@wsu.edu.*

Robert H. Woods, Jr., J.D., Ph.D., has developed online programs for undergraduate and graduate levels. He teaches courses in speech, communication law and ethics, and research. His publishing credits include articles about online education and environments in the *American Journal of Distance Education, Open Learning, International Journal of Instructional Media,* and *Journal of Information, Law and Technology.* He can be reached online at *http://www.arbor.edu/~rwoods* or *rwoods@arbor.edu.*

Samuel Ebersole, Instructional Design Specialist and Professor of Mass Communications at Colorado State University–Pueblo, has been studying new media and the convergence of digital technologies since the late eighties. Professor Ebersole holds a Ph.D. in communications and was awarded an Emmy for his work with NBC Sports coverage of the 1988 Summer Olympic Games. Currently he is researching and teaching about electronic media, interactive multimedia and interface design, and media research. With numerous scholarly articles about media effects and online pedagogy, Dr. Ebersole's research has been cited in the *New York Times* on the Web and the *Christian Science Monitor.* He can be emailed at *ebersole@uscolo.edu.*

Jeffrey Crabill earned a B.S. and an M.S. from Northern Arizona University, then moved to the Seattle area and taught at Everett Community College (EVCC) for three years. While at EVCC, Jeff developed and began teaching mathematics courses online. Currently, Jeff is a mathematics instructor at Linn-Benton Community College in Albany, Oregon. He can be contacted through email at *jeff.crabill@linnbenton.edu.*

Rita Barsun earned a Master of Arts in Teaching at Indiana University–Bloomington (IU-B). She taught French for four years in University School, IU-B's lab school. For more than twenty years, she was an at-home wife and mother, enjoying time with her family and working in her church and in her boys' schools. Volunteering in the school libraries inspired her to become a librarian and she entered IU's School of Library and Information Science in the summer of 1990. She received her Master of Library Science degree in December 1993. In November 1996, at the young age of 55, Rita became the Walden University Liaison Librarian. She can be reached online at *rbarsun@waldenu.edu.*

Leslie Bowman is a career educator and has taught elementary school, college, dance, music, continuing education for private investigators, as well as personal safety, school safety, and self-defense. Her current online teaching includes MSITC courses at Walden University and professional development Educational Technology courses at CaseNex (University of Virginia) and the Institute of Computer Technology. She also teaches personal safety, school safety, bully prevention, and self-defense workshops both online and onsite.

You can contact Leslie online at *http://www.elearningprof.net* or *dlinstructor@yahoo.com*.

Tina Marie Nies is a college instructor and freelance writer with over 11 years of teaching experience. Her online teaching experience includes more than six years teaching at Baker College Online. Tina Marie holds a bachelor's degree in Business Administration from the University of Michigan. Her graduate studies include education, law, and computer information systems. She can be reached online at *tina.nies@baker.edu*.

CHAPTER 1

AN INTRODUCTION TO ONLINE LEARNING

KEN W. WHITE AND JASON D. BAKER

In this chapter, you will learn about:

- One student's experience with online education
- Characteristics of an effective online student
- The needs of an online student

We want to introduce this book with a story. It's a story about one online learner—someone you might relate to. In many ways, Lorraine's story is like the experience of many online students. She went through the public school system and did pretty well. She got average grades, attended regularly, and enjoyed the socializing. But something happened. Unlike other kids, Lorraine dropped out. Why? Maybe it was partly because she was not born into a family that expressed education as a value. Neither of her parents had a high school diploma and education was not emphasized. In some ways, it felt sort of natural for Lorraine to drop out of high school.

Fortunately, dropping out of high school did not prevent Lorraine from getting jobs. In fact, she had many jobs—working in a shoe factory, in a screen print shop, and in a lab looking through a microscope eight hours a day. She finally ended up as a cashier in a retail store.

Then the reality of no high school diploma hit. It turned out that she couldn't advance in this retail organization because of her lack of education. At that time, she thought that was really unfair. Previous to this job, she had been married and had a beautiful little girl. The marriage ended in failure and her life had taken a complete turnaround. Lorraine had become the breadwinner of the family. As a single parent, she needed to step up to the financial responsibilities.

Cashiering was not going to pay enough to support Lorraine and her daughter. She had thought this was going to be the job of her dreams, but the needs of a two-year-old raised the ante. It became necessary that Lorraine move back to her parents' home so that they could watch her daughter during her working hours.

Lorraine needed to get a better job and make more money. She left the cashiering position for a job in the automotive industry. The auto industry paid more, and it didn't require her to go back to school while working on the assembly line. But it was at this time that she became fully aware that she was going nowhere without an education. That was clearly brought home to her by the fact that anytime she was offered a promotion, the opportunity was taken away the moment it was learned that she did not have a high school diploma. She was offered a promotion as a supervisor, but the company required that she get a GED certificate.

It was necessary that Lorraine continue her education. She scrambled to the local high school and took her GED test. Her manager gave her two weeks to pass the GED certificate before completely turning her down for the job. At the time, she considered him the "pushy type." He constantly nagged her about getting a formal education to further her career. He had his master's degree and he did not let up on Lorraine. Lorraine guessed that it was the kind of motivation she needed—she got her GED certificate and immediately signed up at a local college. She began to earn a bachelor's degree by attending classes on Saturdays and Sundays.

Then the obstacles to furthering her education grew. The company closed its facility and Lorraine's hopes of completing a bachelor's degree quickly faded. The firm worked out a transfer for Lorraine, and moved her to a new facility where it seemed like all her associates and fellow employees had master's degrees. She really felt like she didn't fit. In fact, without a bachelor's degree, job opportunities and advancement were definitely not open to her.

Lorraine was faced with a dilemma. Her new job took her on the road a lot and all the local colleges required her to be physically present in classes—not an unreasonable requirement, but one that left her out of the program. Besides that, the closest college was too far away for Lorraine to work and travel to school at the same time.

She was at her wit's end.

Then Lorraine heard about online learning. A fellow employee had read an ad about an online school. Both of them were impressed that even though online education was new, this online program was accredited. It seemed that the program could enable Lorraine both to return to school and to get a legitimate degree. It had many advantages for a person in her situation. For example, Lorraine was always a shy student. The online classroom seemed a perfect place to say things and speak freely about a subject. She found the idea attractive that online, her Eastern accent, as well as many of the features people would normally see and hear in a traditional classroom, would be gone.

Two years later, Lorraine's dream came true as she heard the sound of her name being called up to receive her bachelor's degree. She even delivered the graduation speech for her class in 1994. And that was only the beginning. She decided to keep going and earn a graduate degree as well. As a direct result of online education's flexibility and quality education, she learned that she was up to the challenge and could do it. In another two years, she made a second trip up to the podium and received her master's degree.

Lorraine now teaches online classes for a major learning institution.

What is the moral of the story?

Despite all the obstacles that life, family, and work placed in front of Lorraine, online education offered her a chance for success.

Thanks to the online option, her dream—and yours—can continue.

CHARACTERISTICS OF EFFECTIVE ONLINE STUDENTS

It was not only the online program that helped Lorraine to succeed. As a working adult student with experience and motivation, she had the characteristics for success. She found the online option a perfect fit, though not without significant effort. The online environment allows motivated adult students to return to the classroom and overcome the obstacles that prevent most working adults from attending a traditional college.

Originally, like many people, Lorraine looked at online education as being simply convenient and easy to access. She soon learned that the online environment is challenging because it changes a person's way of thinking. In her exchanges with other online students, she was exposed to how other people handle ideas and problems. The online medium helped her to expand her knowledge by bringing her together with other people. It's a way of learning that gave her new insights and alternative methods for handling problems that she could not learn alone.

On the other hand, it is exactly because of such possibilities and challenges that the online medium is not for everyone. Most online programs are set up for working adults who wish to further their education but are not able to attend a traditional classroom. Consequently, online education requires commitment and particular characteristics of the student. Although online students do not have to be computer experts or have a complete understanding of the software, they do need a willingness to learn.

We think Ronald Gross in *The Lifelong Learner* describes the characteristics of successful online learners to a tee when he outlines some "basic truths" about learning and growth that can strengthen the educational adventure of adult self-development:

- They take command of their own learning, master more things, and master them better than those that rely on being taught. They tend to have greater zest for learning and make better use of their time.
- They learn differently than children do. As working adults, online learners have a different sense of themselves, of their time, and of what's worth learning.
- Adults tend to take responsibility for their own learning. Online learners are able to tailor learning for themselves, not just accept something ready-made.
- How well online learners learn depends, to a great extent, on their temperaments, circumstances, needs, tastes, and ambitions. Success in learning depends not so much on the subject itself (or maybe even on the medium) as on the learner's own engagement.
- Virtually every aspect of the adult online learner's life—work, leisure, personal relationships, and community activities—has the latent power to enhance their learning. But only if the adult learner can find or create the ways to utilize it.

In other words, the working adult who decides on the online alternative needs to take personal responsibility for his or her learning.

You cannot afford to think that online education is an easy way out. If you are planning to attend an online class, you must be self-directed. Online is a tool to assist those who are unable to enter the traditional learning environment, but are motivated to meet their educational goals. As working adult learners, online students bring their goals, experiences, and desire to learn to the classroom. They are motivated to bring something new to each and every class. You must be prepared to succeed.

THE NEEDS OF ONLINE STUDENTS

This handbook is intended to help you succeed in an online classroom. It outlines not only what you have to do to succeed, but also the many ways online programs and teachers can help the working adult online student to succeed.

You should expect certain things from the online program you are considering attending.

For example, online students need support services—support in understanding how a university functions. Online students need to be able to contact an enrollment counselor who can help them through those first few classes. In addition, online students need a social context for learning. Working adults may be self-directed, but they also value the exchange of ideas and meaningful relations. It is particularly important that online programs address these two issues. It is useful if online programs give their students the opportunity to follow the progression of classes in such a way that they will find themselves in classes with the same people, what has been referred to as "learning communities." They are able to develop relationships that enhance their own learning

Online students also need to experience effective online communication and teaching practices. Instructors must help with many technical problems that face the new student. They don't have to fix the problem all the time, just be understanding and know where to refer the student. Online instructors must also give online students a means to contact them other than the over the computer. In many cases, online students with technical difficulties have been required to call a university help desk with a problem because they unable to contact the instructor. Online students should be able to contact the instructor directly by phone if there is some reason they cannot communicate online.

Online students need clear guidance through the online curriculum. Because many online courses are typically all verbal, words must be used effectively. When an online syllabus is prepared, it should be particularly clear and detailed. A detailed explanation of when assignments are due is better understood by students when both the week and the due date of an assignment are referred to rather than just writing, "The assignment is due on Saturday." Syllabi should contain a full description of what is expected when the student is to give feedback to the class. Rather than just tell students, "A summary is due every week," online instructors should tell them exactly what is expected of them in the assignment. The clearer the syllabus, the less likely online instructors will have students coming back and saying, "Oh, I thought you meant . . ."

Online students need an involved instructor. If there is an online student who is not performing, the instructor can send a private note. Encouraging students to talk about how this week's readings apply to their work environment can also stir up some conversation, and keep the online learning process on track. Finally, instructors can let online students know that instructors can and do track attendance in class.

You should expect your online instructor to be visible and involved.

PRACTICAL FRAMEWORK FOR ONLINE LEARNING

The following chapters explore four major areas that online students need to understand and practice. These four areas are:

- Preparation
- The online classroom
- Learning
- Responsibilities

One goal of this handbook is to help you understand the elements of each area and help you successfully perform each task for a more positive, effective online classroom experience. In order to accomplish this goal, the book's chapters will help you address the *preparation* area for online learning by highlighting:

- Communicating with your family and employer
- Creating a personal space for study
- Arranging a consistent schedule
- Using available resources for learning

The *online classroom* area refers to the effort put into helping to create a positive and effective learning environment. The book also highlights:

- Contributing to an online environment of respect and rapport
- Contributing to a culture of learning
- Knowing and following classroom procedures
- Managing your own online behavior

The *learning* area refers to the effectiveness of helping yourself become involved in your online learning. The book will look at such ideas as:

- Being willing and open to learning new ideas
- Asking questions and participating in online discussion
- Applying concepts from the online class to your own experiences
- Offering your opinions and feedback to other online students
- Demonstrating your knowledge of content

Finally, the *responsibilities* area refers to your duties as an online student. They include:

- Reflecting on your learning
- Maintaining a record of your learning
- Communicating with your instructor
- Keeping yourself informed

Each one of these areas will be discussed in the following chapters, offering you ideas, tips, and ways of putting suggestions into practice.

For working adult students, the online method of teaching and learning can far surpass any traditional method. Online students want to get more out of a class than sweating out a final exam. They want practical knowledge and meaningful social interaction. They may be self-directed; but they also want the guidance of a facilitating instructor. If done right, your online experience will instill confidence in you and earn the recognition of others. In short, online education can give you the taste of reward and the personal ful-fillment you never expected.

We hope this book helps you taste that reward and gain that fulfill-ment. New online learning experiences are appearing daily and we hope that *The Student Guide to Successful Online Learning* will help prepare you for a suc-cessful experience.

Good luck!

CHAPTER 2

SO YOU WANT TO BE AN ONLINE STUDENT?

WALLIS C. METTS, JR.

In this chapter, you will learn about:

- How online learning can benefit you
- Challenges of online learning
- Responsibilities of an online student
- Tips for being a successful online student
- Strengths and weaknesses of an online student

So you want to be an online student? Well, there's some good news and there's some bad news. The good news is you can go to class in your pajamas whenever you want. The bad news is you still have to make yourself go. Successful online learning requires self-discipline, organization, sound decision making, and responsibility.

That's the bottom line, as stated in an informal survey of 74 experienced online students with anywhere from one to ten online courses under their belts. Before we examine their experiences and the suggestions they have for you, let's take a brief look at the online phenomenon. It's a promising alternative based on a different view of teaching and learning.

THE PROMISES OF ONLINE LEARNING

The primary promise, of course, for online learning is convenience. Convenience is possible because everyone doesn't have to do everything at the same time. You don't have to be there at 7:45 A.M., or 2:15 P.M., on Monday, Wednesday, and Friday. You can go to class whenever you are able. Night owl? Burn the midnight oil. Early bird? Catch the worm! Is the babysitter sick? Stay home. The online class is always open and you can read the lectures anytime. Through bulletin board style discussions, you can add comments; your instructor post questions; and your classmates make observations anytime. You can respond an hour or even a day later.

Of the students who responded to my survey, nine out of ten said the best part of online learning was flexibility, a function of both time and place. Control over their time was the most common benefit cited by both experienced online students and "newbies." The most common words used to describe online learning were "flexibility," "schedule," "convenient," and, of course, "time." A typical response was, "The best part was that I could go online at anytime—day or night. . . . You work around your own schedule, not someone else's." Another, more visually descriptive student said, "There is something to be said about taking a test in the middle of the night while wearing a pink fuzzy bathrobe and Garfield slippers." Online students definitely like being able to work at home—and said so. Said one working mom, "I like being able to plan my school around my family instead of the other way around." Others liked being able to do their schoolwork at their jobs or even on the road. In a busy world, students liked having control over the time and place they learn.

The *asynchronous* setting of most online educational programs—the anytime, anyplace aspect—also gives you a chance to think more about your responses to discussions. The online students I surveyed found that they made more thoughtful contributions in online conversations than they did in traditional settings. In the online classroom, everyone can participate, bringing a variety of viewpoints to bear on complex issues. For example, one colleague of mine posted a question about the philosopher Kant. He received over 250 responses in less than a week—out of a class of eight students. I have had classes post over a thousand comments in less than three weeks, obviously much more discussion than I might expect in a real-time discussion. Although many online students come to the online classroom for the convenience, they quickly appreciate it for the quality.

On the other hand, another reason online discussions seem to work so well is that there is something comforting about the apparent anonymity. In my informal survey, one student said that the best part was, "The anonymity that allows you to be more truthful and direct without fear of what others will think." Another said, "The best part of taking classes online was the anonymity and the freedom this anonymity carried with it. This freedom allowed me to say what I was truly feeling without the fear of being wrong." Of course, the experience wasn't truly anonymous. Other students in your online class know your name, have your email address, and maybe even know your phone number. But to the online students surveyed, it felt safe and they spoke their minds, without fear of dirty looks or awkward pauses. In an online class, this sense of anonymity can translate into the sort of risk-taking that promotes true intellectual growth and insight. Students who never say a word in the brick-and-mortar classroom make meaningful and insightful contributions online.

THE RESPONSIBILITY OF ONLINE STUDENTS

Online success—your success—depends on your participation. If you do not contribute to the discussion, no one, including the instructor, knows you are there. Although the quality of online discussions results from the fact that you can think about what you say before you say it, and even "say" exactly what you mean, you still have to be there.

You have to be "visible."

The promises and advantages of online learning are balanced by the need for increased responsibility on the part of the student. The thoughtful and sometimes passionate conversation of the online classroom is one reflection of a new learning environment that levels the playing field, and shifts much of the responsibility of learning from the teacher to the student. In the ideal online class, students raise the questions and find the answers with the instructor acting as a mentor and knowledgeable guide. One online student got to the root of the new environment; as she put it, "The best part of taking on an online class is that you have to really dig into the books and information provided in order to learn anything." You have to study. Of course, the best teachers anywhere engage students in the process of discovery, and the best classrooms anywhere are less about lectures (teacher-centered) and more about conversations (student-centered). The online classroom pushes the envelope. It depends on students participating in the process and sharing their discoveries.

THE CHALLENGES OF THE ONLINE CLASSROOM

With all of these promising possibilities, and even with the increased responsibility, your question might be "So what's the problem?" There is no problem, but there are challenges. My brief survey reflected a number of concerns held by online students. Although the online students essentially agreed that the best part of the online experience was the convenience, there is less unanimity about what represents the "worst" part of the experience. Basically, these responses can be divided into three categories: challenges with technology, challenges with self-discipline and organization, and challenges with communication, especially with the instructor. Let's look at each of these challenges.

Technology

Surprisingly, the technology challenge was not the major concern to the online students. Only one-fourth of them mentioned frustrations related to unstable Internet connections, glitches in the online delivery system, or outdated personal computers and software. One student's advice, "Don't try the classes if your Internet connection is prone to failure." As you might imagine, this was particularly frustrating for students who lost connections in the midst of timed tests.

Self-Discipline and Organization

About the same number of students said the "worst" part of their experience was maintaining the organization and discipline necessary to succeed. The freedom to manage one's own time came with the responsibility to do so. "It's easy to fall behind if you aren't disciplined enough," was a typical response. Part of this can be attributed to the environment that can be new and somewhat overwhelming. One student wrote, "It can be confusing to make sure you have all the right assignments and know all the right deadlines. It left me feeling very scattered, but once I organized and figured out a system it was better."

The need for self-discipline in the online classroom is easily the major theme in the advice to someone taking his or her first online course. As one student put it, "You have to manage your own schedule since you are not going to class, and having that constant reminder to get your homework done and study for tests."

Don't procrastinate, log on regularly, and take the class seriously.

Communication

The need for self-discipline, though, was not the "worst" part of the experience in the online students' minds. Remember all those students responding to questions online, and all that insightful commentary? Well, while teachers get absolutely ecstatic over this, students responding to the survey weren't as impressed. Even though communication was frequent and thoughtful, it seemed impersonal. About half said the worst part of the online experience was poor communication. The general issue of communication was frequently characterized as "not being able to communicate directly." The limitations of primarily depending on written communication were mentioned several times. In response to that limitation, online classes are including more audio and video conferencing all the time.

For some students, however, online communication just doesn't seem as satisfying as that which occurs in real time. Even though students respond to other people's ideas, they don't seem to feel like they are responding personally to one another. We are used to having an immediate reaction in our conversations, along with the rich textures of tone and facial expressions, and even body language. In fact a student who exchanges just five emails with the instructor in an entire online course may actually have received more direct feedback than in a traditional classroom setting. But, of course, there was no eye contact or pat on the back. Live online chats do not completely solve this problem, although students who do participate in classroom chats report higher levels of satisfaction than those who don't. Online communication can be frustrating until you get used to it.

Half of those surveyed said they had problems communicating with their instructors. One issue concerned timing, with several complaints about feedback not being "immediate." This lack of immediate feedback is sometimes perceived as a lack of action. In actuality, their real complaint was "waiting for the instructor to respond." One student complained that the instructor only checked her email twice a week. One student wrote, "It can feel very lonely if the professor doesn't respond quickly to your emails."

So remember, online instructors are as varied as those you might have on campus, and not all of them are equally good at communicating with students.

This raises an important point. It is not to yours or to your instructor's advantage for you not to address your concerns about an online class. Don't wait to express your thoughts and feelings in an end-of-the-course survey. It's too late at that point to give your instructor an opportunity to change things and make your experience better.

You need to take responsibility for letting the instructor know what you need in class. Call the instructor at home if you have to.

Of course, some of these challenges are inherent in the system itself. The Internet is interactive—we get what we want immediately or we go somewhere else. This can set up some unrealistic expectations in an online class of 13–25 students. In an online class, we may expect people to be hyperlinked when they are not even logged on. One student wrote, "The worst part was asking questions on the weekend or after hours. I could only email and wait for a response." In this case, the online instructor may not have been responsive or had just taken the weekend off. Although online instructors have the obligation to inform students when they will be away from the computer for any significant length of time, online students often expect immediate responses, something they might not have expected in an offline setting.

Patience is a virtue in the online classroom.

Many of the concerns about online learning address the question of building community. It can and is being done. Just keep in mind, as you enter the online world, you may feel disconnected. It is a natural to feel that way, but it will be a temporary challenge.

THE REWARDS OF ONLINE LEARNING

So, is online learning worth the risk? Yes, it is. Real growth—personal and professional—always involves taking risks. If you are able to accept the new learning environment of student-centered as opposed to teacher-centered education, the rewards can be great. Several students noted this shift and recognized the positive paradox. One student said, "The best part is getting to manage your own schedule and the worst part is having to manage your own schedule." Another student put it this way, "The best part of taking an online class is that you have to really dig into the books and information in order to learn anything. The worst part was 'needing' to dig into the books and information in order to learn something! You really have to be motivated to do your work." This latter online student's advice was "Take it seriously. Don't slack off and think because you don't have to go to class and be seen by the professor that you can do whatever you want and still get a good grade or learn anything. I really liked my online class and probably learned a lot more taking it online than by taking it in a class where I would occasionally daydream or doodle."

In a nutshell, you will gain knowledge, skills, and responsibilities in your online classroom that will translate into other situations, especially to the workplace.

TIPS FOR ONLINE SUCCESS

Here are a few tips for your online success.

Take a Test Drive

Online programs usually have an orientation course, which allows you to become familiar with the features and to test your computer and software. Take it. In fact, one student said, "Take the tutorial twice."

Set a Time and Place

One student writes, "You need a game plan or else things will not get done by the deadlines." This is an idea repeated several times in different ways. "Set aside time every day to go online and get some work done. If you make it a daily habit, it is more difficult to fall behind. . . . Do it at night when there are no distractions." Find a comfortable place in the home where you can work in peace. Let family members know your schedule to discourage interruptions.

Don't Procrastinate

This is exactly how they said it, over and over again. Says one student, "No matter how flexible it is to fit 'going to class' into your schedule, it is still no fun having to finish an assignment the day that it is due." Keep to your schedule, ask questions if you don't understand, and know the syllabus.

Communicate . . . Communicate . . . Communicate

"Establish a rapport with the professor," advises one. Email and ask questions. Check in with your classmates. Attend the chat sessions. Take the initiative and reach out. No one will do it if you don't.

Print the Syllabus

Print the syllabus, assignments, and schedule. Have hard copies of them all. "It often feels like there is more material than there actually is," one student writes. It may be hard to remember where you read about a certain assignment or instruction. Keep a notebook. You can then check assignments offline.

Use Voice Mail

You will be on the computer a lot, and unless you have multiple phone lines or a cable connection, your online class could interfere in other areas of your life. You could miss phone calls that are of immediate importance. You may want to consider voice mail instead of an answering machine. Then you aren't worrying—as one student says she did—that you are missing important calls.

Work Hard

Several students noted that an online class takes the same amount or more work than an on-campus class. One wrote, "Study hard and don't give up." You need to be prepared to increase your daily workload. Ask yourself, do you have the time? Where will you find the time?

Know Thyself

"Make sure you are capable of making yourself do your homework," wrote one student. Another said, "Know what kind of student you are. This takes a lot of discipline." Problems can only be addressed if they are identified. Do you have the "right stuff" to be a successful online student?

Accept Responsibility

A recurring theme, as one online student wrote, was "Hold yourself accountable. Don't blame the instructor if you don't know what is going on. He or she is only an email away." Wrote another, "Only you can make sure that you sign on when you are supposed to and that you do the required work." How committed are you? How proactive?

Relax

"Don't get too uptight," advised one.
    In other words, have fun and enjoy it!

Your Strengths and Weaknesses as an Online Student

List your strengths and weaknesses below as an online student.

STRENGTHS	WEAKNESSES

APPLICATION EXERCISE 2B

Your Decision to Become an Online Student

In order to support your decision to become on online student, respond to the following questions:

- What are your reasons for being an online student?

_____

_____

_____

- Why do you want to take the online option?

_____

_____

_____

- How important is it to you to be an online student?

_____

_____

_____

- What actions do you need to take for your life to best accommodate an online course?

_____

_____

_____

- What time for your online class best fits your schedule?

  _____

  _____

  _____

- What is the best place in the home for you to do your online work?

  _____

  _____

  _____

- What challenges to your online success can you anticipate?

  _____

  _____

  _____

CHAPTER 3

SELECTING AN ONLINE LEARNING PROGRAM

JAMES HOLST

In this chapter, you will learn about:

- Criteria to use when selecting an online program
- Questions to ask about a potential online program
- Choices you need to consider when assessing an online program
- How an online degree may enhance your career

The tide of education is shifting. For years the notion of attending college meant living at a college, or driving to a campus and spending two to four hours a week attending classes. Now the idea of attending college from home or your office is more reality than fiction. Where once it was thought that an education was possible only within a traditional on-campus environment, more and more of us are discovering the online educational approach as another option for obtaining a degree.

Getting a degree in an online environment presents several issues to the potential student. These issues relate directly to the anxiety an online student may feel before, during, and after their educational experience. This anxiety is related to how the student may believe he or she will be perceived by others when pursuing an online degree rather than from a traditional on-campus environment.

In this chapter, I will look at some of the perceptions regarding online education, including choosing a school, potential problems you might face, and how an online degree is accepted once you've graduated. I will also offer suggestions to help you select a program that best addresses these issues.

THE TRADITIONAL AND ONLINE COLLEGE EXPERIENCES

My undergraduate degree was obtained in the way that most people imagine when they think of "going to college." At 18, I enrolled in a state college as a science major. I filled out the proper forms and applied. Within two months I was accepted to the college. After that point, I was willing to accept, sign, and deliver whatever documentation the college required—no fears, no anxieties, no thoughts about whether others would accept my education. I did, however, experience the normal uncertainties about going to a new place and being able to handle the rigors of my educational endeavor.

During college, I attended classes, studied, shared my experiences with others, and really had no significant concerns. I followed the requirements of my major and tried to execute these requirements to the best of my abilities. I gave little thought to how my degree would be received in the "real world." After the prescribed four years (and one extra summer . . . no one's perfect), I graduated with a bachelor's degree in Natural Science. Directly after college, I entered the workforce—confident that my degree was satisfactory for my future needs.

My experience is very typical, as it should be, but I did not have these same feelings as I entered the online environment. In fact, I felt a little stupid applying to a college where I knew I would never meet my advisor, never meet a fellow classmate, and never talk to a professor in person. Why did I feel this way? Among others, the reason that kept popping into my head was "Is this legitimate?" I felt in some ways that I was cheating the system, or perhaps the individuals providing this education were cheating me. I felt that my peers, my family, and my employer would not accept this degree as worthwhile and legitimate.

My concerns had been reinforced many times by peers who were considering the online education route. They asked me, "Do you feel that this education is as solid as any other education?" Or they asked, "Will my employer or future employer accept this education?" With every response I told them nothing but positive things about my experience with the online educational system. I tell them now about the intense interactions between students, the debates, the group assignments, the tests, and the knowledge gained from conversations between a student and instructor, or among students.

An online education is and can be as stimulating, if not more stimulating, than a traditional on-campus education.

Still, there are many online students who feel that they are missing something or are somehow being cheated out of the educational process. I assure you that nothing could be further from the truth. But you must carefully choose the right program to ensure that you receive a quality education.

The quality of your online educational process depends on the choices you make.

RESEARCHING YOUR CHOICE
OF AN ONLINE PROGRAM

At this point, let's say you have decided to move forward with an online education. Like most of us, you are probably asking yourself "What am I getting myself into?" "Can I do this?" "Should I do this?" Great questions. In reality, you would likely be asking these same questions as you begin to move ahead in any educational endeavor. Human nature dictates that we fear the unknown. In many respects, online education is still an unknown. I think we can agree that the concept of online education is no longer a "new" idea. But there is still some fear about whether an online education will be accepted by other schools and employers. You can overcome this fear with just a little homework before you begin. Consequently, your online experience will be a more positive one.

Your first homework assignment is to validate the school and the program that interests you. What do I mean about validation? To be quite honest with you, you must make sure that your school is not a "diploma mill." Please note that most accredited colleges are not diploma mills, but there are some schools that do not meet even basic academic requirements.

First and foremost, you must make sure that your school is accredited.

You should ask your enrollment advisor to send you the school's list of accrediting agencies for which it has current accreditation. Verify that the listed agencies meet the minimum requirements set forth by the United States Department of Education. Validate this information. Do not just take the word of an enrollment advisor. You can find more information about the accreditation process by visiting the United Stated Department of Education web site at *http://www.ed.gov/offices/OPE/accreditation/*.

In the United States there are six regional accrediting agencies that are considered the "gold standard" of institutional quality. When applying to any US-based college, you should make sure that your school is accredited by one of the following agencies:

- New England Association of Schools and Colleges
- Middle States Association of Schools and Colleges, Commission on Higher Education
- Northwest Association of Schools and Colleges
- Southern Association of Schools and Colleges
- Western Association of Schools and Colleges
- North Central Association of Schools and Colleges

Contact a college or university you are familiar with and ask for their accreditation. Then compare their accreditation with the college you are considering. There will be differences. You should compare several colleges to see the similarities and differences between each school. This will give you

TABLE 3.1

	NORTH CENTRAL ASSOCIATION OF SCHOOLS AND COLLEGES	NORTH AMERICAN BUSINESS LEAGUE
University of Phoenix	Yes	No
Arizona State University	Yes	No
World Online University	No	Yes

a good picture of what the school is all about. For example, Table 3.1 helps you to visually compare the differences between schools.

Although all schools may sound legitimate, we can discover some critical factors. For example, one university may not be accredited by one of the big six agencies, or we discover the accrediting agency like the "North American Business League" is not an accredited agency. Knowing this, it would be best to look at other schools.

The second step in our homework is to do a reality check. Remember that there is no such thing as a free lunch.

Look at the online program and see if they are offering you a free lunch. For example, if a school says they can offer a bachelor's degree in three months for students with no prior learning experience, or a doctorate with no residency requirement, perhaps these schools are not appropriate. Remember, if it sounds too good to be true, then it probably is. If a school is a private institution, you can check with organizations such as the Better Business Bureau (*http://www.bbb.org/*) to see if there have been any complaints filed against them.

Simple investigation into an online program can save you many headaches and give you joy when you complete your degree. Take the preceding steps and your fears about your education may be reduced.

WHAT AM I GETTING MYSELF INTO?

Are you wondering, "What am I getting myself into?" There are as many answers to this question as one can imagine, but let's look into some of the more common ones. First, you are getting yourself into your future—where you want your career to go. Or you are getting an education to help you advance into areas where you may not have had access to before. These are all good intentions. However, make sure you are doing this for the right reasons. I have had more than one student enter a program because they wanted to make more money. Is this the only reason to choose a program? Is this the reason you to get into all of this? Perhaps the answer is yes but most likely the answer is no.

Second, your degree choice should have the elements of achievement, fulfillment, and passion.

Although you can obtain the first two elements through hard work, the third one will only come to you if you truly believe in what you are doing.

You may also be asking, "Can I do this?" My first response is that if you enroll in any program, you will want to be sure that you have a foundation. A foundation can come in many forms. In the online environment, the first foundation you must consider is "Can I run a computer?" You may laugh, but many of us did not have computers (that were of any use) in high school or college or perhaps didn't even have exposure to computers at work or at home.

The online environment can be one of the most powerful ways of obtaining an education but you must be able to perform the basics in order to gain from this environment.

The basics include: Can I explain the difference between a file, a directory, and a sub-directory? Do I know how to attach and view files? Do I understand the basics of word processing and presentation software such as Microsoft Office? Do I know how to access email and use the Internet to access information? Answer these questions honestly. If you have answered no to any of these questions, it would be in your best interest to understand and master these basics before starting any online program. Such mastery will help you succeed in this learning environment.

Another foundation question you need to ask yourself is: "Do I have the ability to meet the needs of the degree requirements?"

For instance, if you are looking into a science, business, or engineering discipline, do you have the mathematical abilities to work independently? If you are in a history discipline you may ask, "Do I have the research abilities?" In an online environment you need to ask yourself, "Do I have the writing abilities?" Finally, do you have the time and the commitment to do this program? An online program does save time in that you don't have to travel to the campus or the library. However, do not fool yourself into believing that an online education is any less stressful than any other college education. You will work hard and you will have deadlines. You will need to become somewhat of an expert in time management to make everything work.

Time is a difficult thing to manage. Family, work, and other personal obligations can hamper your efforts. Again, it is up to you to manage your time in a manner that balances all of these factors. It is important for you to find this balance. It will affect you adversely in many ways if you cannot manage this or if you try to find shortcuts. The following is a story of how one of my colleague's students decided not to balance his time. In this particular situation, classes were scheduled from Thursday to Wednesday on a six-week session. I will paraphrase from an email:

> Dear Prof. Tennyson:
>
> I see you have assigned work, which is due on Sunday. I just want to let you know that any homework due on the weekend will be late. I work a second job on Saturdays and alternate Sundays. You will receive my homework on Monday evening. I have other priorities and I have to push my education to later in the week in my situation. Thank you for your understanding.
>
> David

Although one can sympathize with David, Professor Tennyson had to take points off for being late. Why did he do this? The reason is simple: The university schedules classes for intense six-week sessions. The classes do meet during the weekends. In order for Professor Tennyson to teach what is required in the allotted time, he must assign work during the weekend. This student made the choice of not working during the weekend—for a very valid reason—however, the grade this student received, and the education this student received, were greatly diminished because he was not able to manage his time as required for the course.

What could David have done differently to make this work for both him and the instructor?

- Arranged to complete assignments before the due date
- Worked out a schedule with his employer for the necessary time to integrate both work and school
- Reduce responsibilities in other places to have the time for school

You might ask, "Don't you think the student was right and the instructor should have made arrangements to receive the work late from this student?" My answer is no. If this was a class that did not meet on the weekends or was fifteen weeks long, then arrangements might have been made, but in this situation the burden was on the student to meet the requirements.

How can you manage your time in an online environment?

In an asynchronous online environment, look for what I call "lost free time" in your everyday routine.

This can include:

- Getting up half an hour earlier each day and doing homework
- Taking half an hour out of an hour lunch break to do homework
- Making a family homework time with you and your children, helping them as you study
- Looking for things in your life that you can change in order to meet the needs of this new responsibility

Can you do this? You can if you have the right tools.

Be honest with yourself. Ask yourself questions that will make you successful in this program.

Only you know if you can do it.

WILL MY ONLINE DEGREE ENHANCE MY CAREER?

Another major question is: "Will this degree be accepted by my employer, future employers, another educational institution, and my peers?" Let's look at this from what your expectations are once you have completed your degree.

Current Employment

It is very rare to find employment where major changes are going to happen for you immediately after getting your degree. However, it all depends on what you want to achieve with your employer. You may need to position yourself. A degree is one way to position yourself for advancement and stronger economic gain.

Reviews

During a review period some employers look for employee accomplishments outside the typical requirements of the job description. A degree may enhance your position for a raise or growth within the company.

Competitive Job Openings

Maybe that dream job is right in your own backyard but it requires a degree or perhaps a master's degree. Here is your first step in achieving this goal.

Future Employers

Future employers really fall into the same category as your current employer with one big exception. Your degree helps you to get into the door with a potential employer. Ask a human resources representative what they look for when they read a resume in 30 seconds. Among several things, they look for a college degree.

How does this equate with the acceptance of an online degree? Individuals, companies, and military organizations will recognize the work you have done to receive an accredited degree. Look at the successes of those who have received a degree from one university. The University of Phoenix publishes an alumni magazine called *Future*. In the back of this publication you can read about the successes of many students in the online program. These are students who have graduated or are still in degree programs, but have bettered themselves through online education.

For example, I am a person whose online education made a significant difference in my life. In 1995, I was a customer support engineer making a low to moderate salary. In 1997, I received an M.B.A. in Technology Management from an accredited online university. Since that time, I have been commissioned in the United States Naval Reserve after spending my whole career as an enlisted member of the Navy. I have held a management position since 1997, and have taken a position as adjunct faculty with a university. I have also been published in magazines and books, and have tripled my salary, all within five years.

Although it is important to make sure your degree is accredited, the psychology of a degree is another important point. No one has ever questioned my online degree. Rather, they look at me for what I am now, and for what my potential will be for the future. It is also about what you make of the degree. I'm just like most of you—with a family, a job, and a mortgage. Like you, I am trying to make the best of things and looking toward the future. The lesson I learned?

Open your mind to the new frontier of online education—study it, review it, and look for an opportunity to learn and grow.

APPLICATION EXERCISE 3A

Choosing an Online Program

In order to support your decision to choose a particular online program, respond to the following questions.

- Does the online program offer full student services?

  ____
  ____
  ____

- Does the online program give credit for prior learning and experience?

  ____
  ____
  ____

- What kind of computer software and hardware will you need?

  ____
  ____
  ____

- Does the online program have an orientation handbook?

  ____
  ____
  ____

- Will you have an academic adviser? Does that adviser also have recruitment responsibilities? Is it to the advantage of the adviser for you to enroll?

  _____

  _____

  _____

- What assessment tests are you required to take?

  _____

  _____

  _____

- What is the quality of the online program's library?

  _____

  _____

  _____

- How will you get your books and materials?

  _____

  _____

  _____

- Was the online program helpful in finding answers to these questions?

  _____

  _____

  _____

APPLICATION EXERCISE 3B

The Advantages and Disadvantages
of an Online Program

List the advantages and disadvantage of the online program you are considering.

ADVANTAGES	DISADVANTAGES

CHAPTER 4

A TAXONOMY OF
ONLINE COURSES

JASON D. BAKER

In this chapter, you will learn about:

- Some styles of online courses
- Class size, content delivery, and classroom discussion approaches
- How styles of online courses can influence your learning experience
- How to contribute to online discussions

Most of us have spent enough time in traditional classrooms that we know what to expect when we arrive for the first day of class. We're used to the teacher striding to the front of the room, handing out a syllabus, writing notes on the chalkboard, and launching into an introductory lecture. Online courses are different. They differ not only from our experiences with traditional courses but also from one another. You could conceivably take three online courses during a semester and have three radically different experiences. Here are just a few of the different online learning experiences that I had as a student:

- A research course where the majority of the lectures were delivered via videotapes; class discussions were held on a Web-based bulletin board; and the final paper required a team of students using email and telephone conference calls to write and submit a proposal.
- An educational administration course where I was the only student enrolled in the class, and all the course material (e.g., lecture notes, book chapters, articles) was delivered online in electric format.
- A philosophy course that required extensive reading from print books along with weekly written commentaries, and class discussion that occurred in a Blackboard course management system.

- A communication course that used live chat rooms for research and discussion combined with printed workbooks, online articles, and bulletin-board style discussions.

While many people think of online learning as uniform, there are actually many different styles of online courses, and these don't even take into account the varied personalities of the instructors. Courses vary based on their class size, content delivery, and classroom discussion. In this chapter I'll examine each of these three dimensions and explain how they influence the online learning experience. Then I'll discuss how to match the style of course with your learning preferences and offer suggestions for success.

ONLINE CLASS SIZES

Online courses range in size from a single student to hundreds of students. The four most common sizes of online classes can be categorized as independent studies, tutorials, seminars, and audiences. The number of students in a course will have a noticeable effect on the learning experience.

In independent study courses you learn with little to no contact with other students or the instructor. Typically you receive course materials at the beginning of a course, including lectures, books, and assignments, and then you work through the material at your own pace. These materials may all be online, or a combination of offline and online materials. Furthermore, the actual instruction may be completely computer-led, with online simulations and computer-graded exams, or may be instructor-led with assignments being turned in via email or the Web. The advantage of this approach is that you can usually work at your own pace (although some college courses set time limits for course completion) and study whenever is convenient. The primary disadvantage is that you lose the feedback of fellow classmates and, very likely, regular interaction with the instructor. Another disadvantage is that most independent study courses are "canned," meaning that each lesson has already been written, and there's little customization based on student needs or desires.

Tutorial-style courses have small class sizes, typically one to three students, and involve a greater level of interaction with the instructor. The tutorial model attempts to offer more frequent interaction between the instructor and the learner, along with the potential of learner-to-learner interaction, while still maintaining the time and subject flexibility associated with independent studies. Unlike most independent studies, however, tutorials are often customized to the needs of individuals or groups of students using a learning contract. Learning contracts are usually written by the students, under the guidance of the instructor, and outline the learning objectives, content materials, and assessment tasks that will be undertaken throughout the course. Since you're involved in the creation of the tutorial course, you have greater control over the packing and content of the course when compared to larger courses. In most tutorials, you maintain regular contact with the instructor, often through weekly or monthly dialogues in which you discuss your learning activities. Other tutorials facilitate such interaction by requiring you to submit each assignment as you complete it, giving time for the instructor to grade and return it prior to meeting.

Seminar-style courses are probably the most common online courses, at least on the university level, and generally involve three to twenty students. The size is large enough to support robust class discussion, but yet small enough to still permit personal interaction with the instructor. In many respects, online seminars are not dramatically different from offline ones—seminar instructors often structure the courses identically to face-to-face ones except, of course, that communication takes place online. Class discussions, often taking place using electronic bulletin boards and sometimes in chat rooms, are commonly used in seminars. This approach offers students the chance to interact with one another as well as the instructor throughout the duration of the class. This not only improves the learning experience, but it greatly decreases the feeling of isolation often associated with distance learning. The drawback to seminars is that they limit the student who wants to move through a program at a different rate, either faster or slower, than the academic calendar permits.

Audience courses have large class sizes—twenty or more students—and may even enroll hundreds of students simultaneously. In many respects, audience courses are the online equivalent of campus courses delivered in large lecture halls. Such courses can reduce the opportunities for personal interaction, though sometimes the course is divided into small groups with facilitators (think recitations with teaching assistants), and functions more like an online seminar. The challenge for many in audience-style courses is that they may feel less like students and more like spectators. Although this feeling may occur when sitting in the back of a large lecture hall, at least you're in an academic building, whereas when you're online, you're one click away from CNN. The advantage of audience courses is that they often provide the best opportunity to learn from leading scholars who might not otherwise be accessible. They're also beneficial to those who really enjoy the lecture hall model.

Table 4.1 summarizes the advantages and disadvantages of various online class sizes.

TABLE 4.1   **Comparison of Online Class Sizes**

CLASS SIZE	DESCRIPTION	ADVANTAGES	DISADVANTAGES
Independent study	Single student	Can learn at own pace	Can feel isolated
Tutorial	One to three students	Personal attention from the instructor; team learning opportunities	Not as time-flexible as independent study
Seminar	Three to twenty students	Potential for significant class discussion while still engaging the instructor	As the size increases, online discussions can get overwhelming
Audience	More that twenty students	Large support system of fellow students; can result in high-quality class discussion	Can feel distant from the instructor

ONLINE CONTENT DELIVERY

Online courses use a variety of online and offline technologies to deliver course content. Although one might imagine that courses touted as web-based are completely online, the reality is that instructors choose to deliver materials in ways best suited to learning. For example, why would someone choose a web site if there's an excellent (printed) book already available? Similarly, why settle for print when a good video segment or computer animation would convey the material far more effectively? As a result, you'll find a mixture of technologies in online courses, including printed and electronic text, presentation graphics, audio/videocassettes and streams, video conferencing, simulations, and virtual reality.

Most online courses incorporate a lot of reading. Textbooks, workbooks, journals, novels, magazines, articles, and individual handouts are used at least as often, if not more, in online courses than in campus-based courses. While face-to-face classes often contain lectures in addition to the books, some online courses increase the amount of reading to compensate for the lack of an online lecture. Typically, you receive a book list at the beginning of the class, and then the syllabus or study guide leads you through the required readings. Sometimes all of the reading materials will be bound into a series of course-specific volumes and purchased at the beginning of the course.

Electronic publishing is growing in popularity and beginning to offer a significant alternative to print publishing. Although it's unlikely that you'll be discarding your printed textbooks in the near future, as an online student you will likely encounter a number of electronic publications during your studies. Adobe Acrobat files, the de facto standard for electronic document delivery, are often used by individual faculty looking to provide electronic copies of articles or notes. Acrobat produces an electronic copy of a document, including text, graphics, and photos, that looks and prints identically to the original version (including hand-written comments, highlights, and heavy creases). Acrobat can also work with optical character recognition to produce a cleaner and searchable copy of the article. Some online libraries use Acrobat to provide an electronic reserve collection for enrolled eLearners.

Electronic course packs are another example of electronic texts that you're likely to encounter. Instructors submit required reading lists (e.g., journal articles, Web sites, and personal notes) to a publisher who then produces electronic reading packets that contain all of the materials in electronic form. These electronic volumes are often Adobe Acrobat PDF files or one of the eBook formats, and offer a low-cost, easy-to-update, searchable alternative to bound paper. Electronic library databases also offer a tremendous resource for online learners. If you take online courses from a university, you're likely to receive access to many electronic databases such as Lexis-Nexis, PsycINFO, Dow Jones Interactive, and Britannica Online. Not only can you search through the contents and abstracts of thousands of periodicals, you're often able to view the full texts of the articles.

One way that some instructors present material online is through presentation graphics packages such as PowerPoint. Sometimes these presentations are annotated with streaming audio, but often they are soundless presentations. While such presentations lack the in-depth content found in other media, they often provide an overview of the key points found in the readings for that week. Many instructors incorporate these slides into online courses in lieu of traditional lectures. For those instructors interested in preserving lectures, audio and video presentations fit the bill. Audio and videotapes are often a holdover from the pre-Web distance learning days, but they are used to supplement some online courses. Audiocassette lectures have a number of advantages over other delivery methods. Cassette tapes are inexpensive, portable, and personal.

I can recall driving to work listening to a series of tapes that supplemented an online communication course I was taking. Although the tapes that I heard were a series of expert interviews that had been conducted in a sound studio and professionally edited, some instructors simply tape their regular in-class lectures for their online students. Similarly, videotaped or televised lectures are sometimes used to enhance online courses. More sophisticated courses stream the audio and video via the Internet, rather than shipping tapes to students, but this requires a stable (and preferably high bandwidth) connection on your end. Although streaming audio works with most connection speeds, if you're still accessing the Internet with a dial-up modem, you would be advised to avoid classes that make extensive use of streaming video.

Packages such as NetMeeting make it possible to conduct full-motion video conferencing courses online, but they are more common in corporate training programs where everyone is on a high-speed corporate network. Video conferencing opens up the possibility of an online learning experience quite similar to a face-to-face one, with the students watching the instructor live, asking questions, and mingling with fellow classmates. Most online conferencing is one-way (typically with the students watching the instructor), but if everyone has high-speed connections it is possible for everyone to appear live and in person. Although the multisite approach is more common in a corporate training program or multicampus university system (where the high-speed network is already in place), one-way instructor video combined with two-way (or multipoint) graphics, whiteboard, and audio is growing in popularity.

Computer-animated simulations and virtual reality aren't incorporated in many online courses at the present time, but can significantly enhance the learning experience when they are used. Computer-animated simulations can be used to add depth to many subjects, from math and physics to art and history, and are most frequently used as supplements to text-based material. An increasing number of textbooks are including online companion sites with such rich media resources that online instructors are using. In addition, rudimentary virtual reality services such as Multiple User Dungeons (MUDs) and Object Oriented MUDs (aka MOOs) offer the opportunity to learn in computer-generated environments customized for the online learning experience. These are largely text-based virtual worlds that serve as the online environment for learning. For example, an instructor might create a MUD with a lecture hall, library, laboratory, and coffeehouse. Students would then login to the MUD and listen to the instructor speak in the lecture hall, read the latest electronic articles in the library, work with a simulation of a frog dissection in the lab, and then chat with fellow students in the online coffeehouse. While this is a far cry from the virtual reality experiences found in the movies, it's nevertheless a creative online learning experience and the first step toward a richer virtual environment.

There is no ideal approach to presenting content; each approach has its advantages and disadvantages, as seen in Table 4.2.

TABLE 4.2   Comparison of Instructional Delivery Styles

INSTRUCTIONAL DELIVERY	DESCRIPTION	ADVANTAGES	DISADVANTAGES
Text	Book learning, either traditional or electronic form	Familiar; packs a lot of content into the course	Audio and visual learners at a disadvantage
Presentation Graphics	Use of PowerPoint-style presentations	Good for overview of material	Generally lacks the depth of more textual presentation
Audio and Video	Audio or video on tape or via online streaming	Richer content than with text alone; tape-based material is portable	Poor production values can hinder learning; may simply stream existing lectures rather than design courses for online delivery
Video-conferencing	Live video delivery	Very similar to a traditional classroom experience	Requires high bandwidth or everything gets choppy
Simulations	Computer-animated materials	Valuable for visual subjects	Requires robust computer systems and high bandwidth to work well
Simulations and virtual reality	Computer-based worlds for instructional experience	Can create a more conducive learning environment than a classroom	Difficult to create; high learning curve for students to understand how the system works

ONLINE CLASSROOM DISCUSSION

Unless you're enrolled in an independent study, communication with the instructor and with fellow students is an important part of the online learning experience. There are four basic approaches to such classroom discussion: none, audio or video conferencing, synchronous online chat, and asynchronous online discussion. As you may guess, the class size and instructional delivery methods chosen often influence which interaction model is selected.

The first approach to classroom discussion is to have none. Yes, it's true, some online courses don't have any classroom discussion. This may be by design, as in the case of most independent study courses, or it may be because the instructor is too busy to participate. I once took an online course where we didn't hear from the instructor for weeks. Students started emailing and calling each other trying to figure out if we were the only ones confused. Needless to say, it wasn't planned this way and the silence detracted from the online learning experience. Obviously, one must be a good independent learner to profit without class discussion—it best suits those who would prefer to simply interact with the material and then take tests, write papers, and demonstrate their mastery of the course content.

Some online courses make use of Internet phone services or offline conferencing resources to add audio or video conferencing for class discussion. This approach generally requires students be online (or by their telephone) at a scheduled time in order to participate in class discussion. The benefit, however, is a rich class discussion that closely emulates a face-to-face experience. Similarly, some courses incorporate live chat rooms to foster live classroom discussion. Chat rooms are the computer equivalent of a conference call—everyone in the class gets online at the same time, and then logs on to a chat room for discussion. Instead of speaking to one another with voices, you type your entire interaction. This works best if you're a fast typist.

As pointed out in Chapter 2, asynchronous discussions are the most common approach to online class discussion. These interactions are time-delayed, much like the message postings on a bulletin board, and don't require that everyone is online at the same time. You post your message onto a discussion board at a time convenient to you, and then others read it when they are online and post their response. Since students don't have to be online at the same time, you can participate in class discussions whenever it is convenient for your schedule. Furthermore, if you're the type of person who needs time to consider a question before answering, this gives you the chance to do so. This approach also provides an archive of all discussions throughout the course. You can reference or resume any conversation throughout the course. Although asynchronous discussions lack the spontaneity associated with live interaction, the advantages far outweigh the disadvantages for many students.

There are advantages and disadvantages to each of these discussion approaches, as seen in Table 4.3.

TABLE 4.3   Comparison of Interaction Types

INTERACTION	DESCRIPTION	ADVANTAGES	DISADVANTAGES
None	No interaction	Benefits independent learners	Missing the insights of fellow students
Audio/video conferencing	Live audio or video discussion	Lively group discussions	Can be costly
Synchronous online chat	Computer chat room	Low cost, real-time interaction	Slower than verbal chats
Asynchronous online discussion	Email or message boards	Everyone doesn't have to be connected simultaneously; archive of discussions	Less spontaneous than live chats

SELECTING A SUITABLE STYLE

It's important to recognize that the variety of online courses means that not all online learning experiences will be identical. There is no single "best" model, and you may not always find your desired degree program offered using the exact combination of class size, content delivery, and classroom discussion that you prefer. I've seen first-hand what happens when students enroll in a course with one instructional style in mind, only to find that the instructor designed the course using another. Some of these students have really struggled with the mismatch of their expectations with the actual course style. Therefore, consider which approaches work best for your circumstances and learning styles, and then select a program that offers the closest fit to your ideal.

APPLICATION EXERCISE 4A

■ ■ ■ ■ ■ ▬▬▬▬▬▬▬▬▬▬▬▬▬▬▬▬▬▬▬▬▬▬▬▬▬

Identifying Positive Discussion Roles

Some form of group discussion is common to most online courses, and it is useful to reflect on how you can effectively participate. Group members play either positive roles that enhance discussion or negative roles that detract from discussion. For example, the *Initiator* is willing to get a discussion started; the *Supporter* encourages the participation of others; the *Mediator* attempts to relieve tension; the *Clarifier* asks questions that clarify meaning; and the *Synthesizer* brings ideas together into themes and main ideas. Negative roles include the *Aggressor*, who attempts to dominate discussions and often antagonizes others; the *Appeaser*, who withholds input and denies his or her own point of view; the *Distracter*, who keeps the group off the subject or task; and the *Dehumanizer*, who ignores other people's feelings in order to accomplish the task.

After your first few online discussions, list the positive and negative roles you played in those discussions:

POSITIVE ROLES	NEGATIVE ROLES
_____	_____
_____	_____
_____	_____
_____	_____
_____	_____
_____	_____
_____	_____
_____	_____
_____	_____

CHAPTER 5

COMMUNICATING IN THE ONLINE CLASSROOM

KEN W. WHITE

In this chapter, you will learn about:

- Communication issues in the online classroom
- The challenges of online communication
- How to communicate the WRITE WAY online
- The "netiquette" of online communication

As a new online student, you are now exposed to the new technology of the electronic classroom. Computer-mediated technology and networking are changing the way people learn and the way they communicate in school. Members of learning teams use computer networks to communicate with one another and to access databases. Online students and groups communicate through electronic mail, distribution lists, and bulletin boards. Computer-based communication may prove to be more significant than the personal computer revolution of a few years ago. Because the technology is used for communication, it affects the most critical process in learning and education.

I know that you want to succeed in the online classroom and that you appreciate how that means effective attitudes and communication skills. This chapter is devoted to tips that can help you communicate effectively with the new technology of computers, specifically email. This is a social view of computer-based communication. I do not consider the technical details, but how the technology requires special ways of thinking, relating, and communicating. My purpose is to help you to see how the changes of new technology can be capitalized on from a communication perspective. If you take these ideas to heart, you may be able to avoid many of the mistakes other students have made in the online learning environment.

I will start with some background information that relates the area of new technology to communication.

COMMUNICATION AND THE ONLINE CLASSROOM

If you want to stay current in the classroom, you need to learn how to communicate effectively with computer technology. Futurists predict that information and access to it will be the basis for literacy in this century. Whether you want to exchange information with other online students or with co-workers, the new technology will be your tool.

Email is a good example. It is a very powerful information tool that is simple to use and easy to understand. It is hard to imagine any other form of computer-based communication that can be so intimate and yet so wide reaching—so focused and so expansive. An online student can communicate as easily with someone from another school across twelve time zones as with another student in the same building.

Lee Sproull and Sara Kiesler, researchers of online behavior, recognize the major challenge of technology like email. They emphasize that such technologies have both *efficiency effects* and *social effects*. Faster and easier communication is not always better social communication. Because an online message is easier to send, students may be tempted to "speak" before they think, and injured relationships may result.

Communicating with computer technology is not simply a matter of adding hardware and software to a learning institution. Online communication leads to communicating and relating in new ways, and thereby to fundamental changes in how students and educators work and relate. In the following section, I outline some of the other challenges of computer-based communication.

THE CHALLENGE OF ONLINE COMMUNICATION

The challenge of communicating online is the inherent complexity of any human communication and interpretation. Even if the recipient of face-to-face communication fully understands what our words mean, misunderstanding can still occur because of faulty assumptions. The words we communicate may be understandable; however, the "why" may be fuzzy.

People are constantly involved in a type of "cognitive shorthand" as they strive to make sense of those around them. Online communicators are particularly prone to faulty assumptions because online communication excludes rich and significant cues on which people normally rely as information sources. Nonverbal cues are a dominant source of meaning in interpersonal communication. Electronic conversations are missing body language and voice intonations, crucial elements of effective communication. When we take these elements away, people are forced to "fill in the blanks." Online communicators can "fill in the blanks" with faulty assumptions, and blow things entirely out of proportion.

Online communicators can come out of "left field" with surprising and often insulting language. "Onliners" refer to this type of communication as *flaming*. Flaming can be defined as electronic messages or retorts that express startlingly blunt, extreme, and impulsive language because the technology lacks tangible reminders of the audience. Faulty assumptions usually lie behind every flame. A writer receives a message open to interpretation, lacks the nonverbal and paralinguistic resources to help interpret the ideas appropriately, assigns faulty assumptions to the message, and reacts with anger and name-calling. When this happens, everything can go downhill fast.

How do we reduce the likelihood of faulty assumptions and flaming in our online classroom? As a general guideline, improving the quantity and quality of communication can reduce faulty assumptions and a flaming mindset. A general point is that online communicators should check out assumptions more frequently and ask a lot more questions than they normally do in day-to-day interpersonal communication.

I conclude this section with an outline of other—not necessarily good, not necessarily bad—aspects of online communication of which you should be aware:

- *Students and groups communicating in a computer-mediated environment are relatively more uninhibited.* "Flaming" is only one outcome of this dynamic. Online students and group members are also more willing to disclose personally sensitive information about them relative to face-to-face interaction.
- *Status differences play a lesser role in an online classroom.* The fact that a person is The Teacher or The Professor or Knows What He or She Is Talking About has a less inhibiting effect on interaction. As a consequence of the low level of social information, online students lose their fear of social approbation. On the other hand, interaction in online groups tends to be more evenly distributed among group members.
- *Online consensus decision making takes significantly longer than when group members interact face to face.* It tends to be more difficult for online students to reach agreement. One difference is that tendencies to be interactive and outspoken in electronic discussions sometimes lead to increased group conflict. Such divergence means that electronic groups have to exert more effort trying to reconcile contradictory opinions than in face-to-face work groups.

The next section will build on the discussion of the nature of communication, online and otherwise, to include techniques for improving the quality of online communication. I will cover techniques—borrowed from traditional training material and adapted for online—intended to improve information and understanding and to lessen faulty assumptions among online students.

THE *WRITE WAY* TO COMMUNICATE ONLINE

The purpose of this section is to move from a general understanding of principles to the application of ideas in the online classroom. To begin with, acronyms are helpful to remember useful concepts. In thinking through what's important in online communication—given problems such as the absence of nonverbal cues, inaccurate assumption, and so forth—University of Phoenix online instructor Chad Lewis has come up with an acronym that covers the essential skills of online communication. He calls it the *WRITE WAY* to communicate online.

The *WRITE WAY* to communicate online involves communicating in a manner that is W(arm), R(esponsive), I(nquisitive), T(entative), and E(mpathetic). Following is an explanation of each component of the WRITE WAY.

W(armth)

Words on a screen are two-dimensional. Reading these words in isolation of usual communication cues lends itself to "coolness" that can lead directly to overreaction and flaming. Essentially, the goal is to interact with people, not with computers. In addition, online students sometimes lose perspective, acting as though messages are going into the relative privacy of a text file saved to the user's hard drive rather than being downloaded and read by an entire class. In turn, these people read two-dimensional words in isolation and react. Pretty soon it's . . . BOOM! Communication leads to embarrassment, chagrin, guilt, shame, and anger—in short, to potentially counterproductive human emotions.

Increasing warmth of online communication doesn't mean to be "touchy feely," to give people the online equivalent of sloppy hugs and kisses. Rather, increasing warmth means to decrease the psychic distance among classmates and the instructor. Being warm online is a way of affirming relational communication; it is about communicating with people.

In short, words can be "cold." We need to find effective ways to warm them up when communicating online. Here are ways to increase electronic warmth:

1. *Use the telephone when necessary.* A telephone call to clarify a point or to negotiate a particularly sensitive issue is indicated when text just doesn't cut it. Some onliners think electronic messages should suffice for all communication, but an occasional phone call can be useful. I see this in the common revelation experienced when phoning someone with whom I have been communicating online. Invariably, the confirmation that we are all human and not just words on a screen is the first thing discussed when voice connection is made.

2. *Send sensitive information to private mailboxes*. It's usually much more helpful to offer "constructive feedback" privately. This approach is akin to offering feedback behind closed doors. Some concerns about the class or classmates are best sent to the instructor's private mailbox.

3. *Incorporate warmth into the written text*. Professional writers are able to convey a wide range of emotions. It is much tougher for beginning online students to do this. I have found it helpful to occasionally write about families and interests. Sometimes I tell a bad joke. Describing the setting from which you are writing, the weather or the music to which you're listening can help other online students and the instructor place you in a human setting.

Playing with language and its symbolism also adds warmth as long as it is not overdone. One way to play with language and symbols online is to use an occasional *emoticon* in your writing. Emoticons represent a way of bringing so-called "nonverbal" cues into online communication though, technically, they are not "nonverbal" communication in the usual sense of the word. Authentic nonverbal communication is beyond our control. It is not necessarily a conscious effort to communicate a particular meaning and it is readily open to other people's interpretations.

Emoticons are conscious and ask the reader to accept a certain tone or meaning. Emoticons, because they are conscious symbols with intent, cannot be trusted like true nonverbal communication, but they do serve a purpose online. As part of a long-term relationship with established trust, they can warn readers not to misinterpret certain words. Table 5.1 lists some of the more common ones.

TABLE 5.1   Emoticons and Their Meanings

1.	:-)	User smiling	11.	:-&	User tongue-tied
2.	:-(	User sad	12.	:-t	User cross
3.	:-<	User very sad	13.	:-@	User screaming
4.	:-\	User undecided	14.	:-x	User lips sealed
5.	:-p	User sticking tongue out	15.	:-e	User disappointed
6.	:-D	User talks too much	16.	::-)	User wears glasses
7.	:-o	User surprised	17.	;-)	User winking
8.	:-O	User shocked	18.	(-:	User left-handed
9.	:-{	User has mustache	19.	>:-<	User mad
10.	:-I	User has no expression	20.	I-)	User bored

R(esponsiveness)

As already stated, "asynchronous communication" means online students sometimes wait several hours before getting a response to a message. Not only is there a lack of the usual communication cues, but there is also the need to wait for feedback. This waiting can feed into invalid assumptions ("The instructor hasn't replied! Hmmm . . . guess he doesn't really think much of my ideas"). A misinterpretation seems to be magnified by the passing of time and can be blown up into a major problem.

Solutions include:

1. *Set deadlines or otherwise be consistent in terms of when you respond to other online students or instructors.* Generally speaking, try to return messages as soon as possible. Time is a particularly important nonverbal for email communication. Online attitudes toward responsiveness are communicated by the ways individuals deal with time. If they are late with their replies, they send a message of indifference to others.
2. *Remember to provide occasional reminders.* Another aspect of responsiveness is redundancy. Think of issuing reminders as a proactive type of responsiveness. An interesting aspect of online communication is that it is possible to have a perfect memory of what was "said." Unfortunately, it is difficult to access a recollection if it is buried in hundreds of kilobytes of information. Consequently, don't be surprised if people fail to act on an online request, particularly if information is part of a larger message or part of a succession of messages on related topics. The use of short messages and redundancy helps to allay this problem and keeps online communicators on track.

I(nquisitiveness)

Defensiveness is reduced if online students ask questions rather than make statements. It is usually more constructive to ask a person "why" than it is to tell them "what." Inquisitiveness serves two important purposes: besides reducing defensiveness, it often provides information that is useful for solving a problem, resolving an issue, or whatever. Bringing valid information to bear on online communicative exchanges is almost always a good idea.

- *Be sure to ask questions.* Online defensiveness tends to be reduced when people ask questions rather than make statements.

T(entativeness)

Defensiveness is reduced when people hear or read "It appears that . . ." as opposed to "It is . . ." Inquisitiveness and tentativeness work well together.

A question, framed in a tentative manner, reduces defensiveness and can also contribute valuable information (e.g., "Don't you think it'd be better if we . . . ?").

- *Use tentative language and posturing, unless the situation dictates otherwise.* The old concept of sending "I" rather than "you" messages works as well in online writing as it does in oral interaction. It is often better to say or to write "I believe . . ." rather than to say or write "You are . . ."

Sometimes you must make absolute statements. You must occasionally send "you" messages. When to be absolute and when to be tentative is up to you. It is a judgment call.

E(mpathy)

An important aspect of online communication is to:

- *Put yourself in the shoes of the other online students and your instructor.* Always consider your online audience. There are a wide variety of issues to keep in mind. For example, a person can be a highly effective, intelligent contributor to an online class even if he or she misspells words or doesn't write well. Remember that there is a difference between an online class discussion and a formal written assignment.

To summarize this section, the *WRITE WAY* to communicate in the online classroom involves communicating in a manner that is W(arm), R(esponsive), I(nquisitive), T(entative), and E(mpathetic).
W(armth) means to:

- Use the telephone when necessary.
- Send sensitive information to private mailboxes.
- Incorporate warmth into text.

R(esponsiveness) means to:

- Set deadlines, or otherwise be consistent, in terms of when you respond.
- Remember to provide occasional reminders.

I(nquisitiveness) means to:

- Be sure to ask questions.

T(entativeness) means to:

- Use tentative language and posturing, unless the situation dictates otherwise.

E(mpathy) means to:

- Put yourself in the shoes of your online classmates and instructor.

THE NETIQUETTE OF ONLINE COMMUNICATION

There is such a thing as proper "netiquette" in the online classroom. It is easy enough to use email but, as you have seen, there is an art to communicating effectively online. I conclude this chapter with a few additional tips from a 1994 post from *Time* magazine's Web site for making friends and influencing people, applicable to the online classroom:

- *Keep your messages brief and to the point (unless it is a work assignment where your teacher asks for important details and examples).* If you want to make sure people listen to what you have to say, do not bore and confuse them with rambling messages that tend to be skipped in favor of shorter messages that concentrate on one subject. Stick to the subject of that particular discussion.
- *If you are responding to a message, quote the relevant and specific passage or summarize it for those who may have missed it.* Do not make other students or the instructor guess what you are talking about, especially if you are responding to a particular message. Highlight the message that you are responding to right up front (often with a symbol like >) and then follow with your response. One example:

  > What time do you want to meet tomorrow?
  Mike—2:00 PM will be fine. See you there! Sue

- *Don't start a "flame war" unless you are willing to take the heat.* Just as you shouldn't drive when you are angry, you should not send email responses when you are mad at someone. Go ahead and type a response, but do not mail it until the next day. Chances are that when you come back later to read your response, you'll be glad that you did not send it.
- *Never copy someone else's writing without permission or citation.* Acknowledge your sources. Define the difference between what others have written and what you think. State your own contribution.

- *Don't clutter discussions with short "I agree" and "Me too!" messages.* It is very frustrating to find lots of messages with very little substance. Remember that email communication can be "labor-intensive" and that it takes time to read numerous messages.
- *Don't type in all caps. (IT'S LIKE SHOUTING!)* You can do it once in a while for strong emphasis, but only for individual words.
- *Don't flame people for bad grammar or spelling errors.* Spelling and correct grammar are important, but online communication tends to be informal. Even though sloppy messages that are full of errors stick out, the principle of constructive feedback that says effective feedback is solicited should be followed.

Now go ahead and enjoy your online learning experience!

Guidelines for Writing Effective Online Messages

In order to judge whether an online message is appropriate, respond to the following questions:

- Is the message direct? Are you leaving out words? Are you assuming something about the receiver that maybe you shouldn't?

_____

_____

_____

- Should the messages be sent immediately or delayed? Are you angry when you write it? Can you wait 24 hours? Does the receiver need this information immediately?

_____

_____

_____

- Is the message clear? Are you asking a question when you really should be making a statement? Or are you making a statement when you really should be asking a question? Is the message congruent with your other messages?

_____

_____

_____

- Is your message "straight"? Is the stated purpose of the message the same as its real purpose? Is there a hidden agenda? Why are you writing this to the other person? Do you want the receiver to read this or something else?

_____

_____

_____

- Is the message supportive? Are you avoiding "global labels" and writing about specifics? Are you avoiding sarcasm? Are you making negative comparisons? Is your message judgmental? Are their any emotional threats?

_____

_____

_____

CHAPTER 6

TOURING THE ONLINE CLASSROOM

CLIFF LINES AND DORIS E. SWEENEY

In this chapter, you will learn about:

- The major elements of an online class
- The qualities of online discussion participation
- Your own time and life management issues

Online learning is different and it's exciting. To help prepare for your first excursion into the cyber classroom and online education, we've put together a tour of a typical online classroom with an explanation of what might be expected of you in an online class. As we've already learned, there are a variety of models of online courses. This tour focuses on an asynchronous learning experience using a commercial courseware platform such as Blackboard. Let's get started.

THE ONLINE COURSE HOME PAGE

The course home page will be the first stop on our tour. This will probably be the first page that you'll see when entering your course. The course developer will probably have designed this page with features to encourage many return trips. What exactly are you going to see? At a minimum, you will find the course title and course number. Material found on this page tends to be dynamic, such as announcements, schedule, and syllabus changes, so you'll want to check it often. In the Blackboard management system the course home page defaults to the announcement page, so you can quickly see the latest messages posted by your instructor. Along the left-hand side of the screen are a series of navigational links to the rest of the course, featuring sections such as: Announcements, Syllabus, Faculty Information, Course Materials, Assignments, Discussions, and Groups.

Online students "logon" to their classes at any time of the day and night. Some prefer to do this first thing in the morning, others during the workday or in the evenings. We often check our courses in the mornings before going to work, but usually wait until the evenings to devote significant time to school work. It's useful to know what time zone your online instructor is working in. You may find that your instructor posts on a set schedule—early morning or after lunch. Keep in mind that online instructors benefit from the same flexibility that you do, and may be doing class maintenance (checking on your class discussions and doing their own posting as appropriate) at all times of the day and night. During the morning, you might check for any late-breaking announcements. The announcements can range from reminders of upcoming assignment due dates to revisions of the syllabus. Online instructors occasionally adjust assignment due dates. If you're not paying attention, you might miss out on a needed extension for that monster end-of-semester project.

So check for announcements every time you logon.

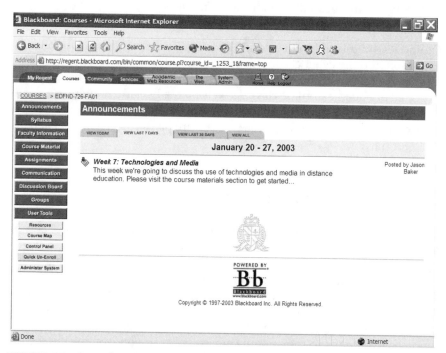

FIGURE 6.1   Sample "Announcements" page.

THE ONLINE SYLLABUS AND SCHEDULE

The online class syllabus will be very similar to what you're used to seeing in a face-to-face class. It'll have a brief description of the course as well as objectives, policies, and grading criteria. You should also see a schedule for the course with assigned readings, activities, assignment descriptions, and due dates. This is a very important document and one you'll want to refer to regularly. We recommend that you print this one out for easy reference, read this document carefully all the way through, and review it online periodically for any changes. Your success in the online class depends upon it. A typical syllabus will provide the following:

- An overview of the course
- Course goals and objectives
- Text information
- Guidelines for each week of the course
- Requirements for assignments, readings, individual, and group projects
- Resource information
- Online instructor contact information
- Guidelines and due dates for assignments

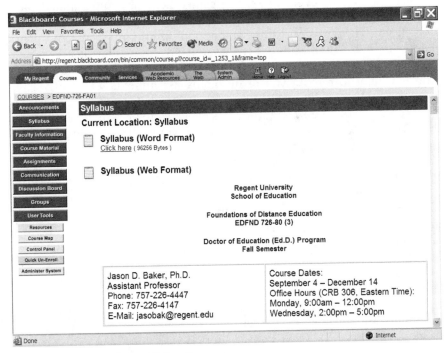

FIGURE 6.2 Sample "Syllabus" page.

- Writing guidelines and style requirements
- Grading criteria for late assignments or lack of participation
- Technical support

It is important to use the syllabus to help set your daily schedule throughout the term. You will need to do the "regular" things you usually do, but as an online student, you will also need to plan to attend to the requirements for the course each day whether you read a few pages, reply to a discussion question, take notes, or conduct research. By understanding the syllabus and using it to coordinate a schedule, you will be able to move forward with course projects, and still be able to find some time to go to a movie or take a walk on the beach.

A calendar will help you keep track of the starting and ending dates of different online courses. Tracking dates will help you to develop a timeline. At the start of every course, we review the syllabus carefully, adding due dates for assignments and important events such as a video or phone conferences into our calendars. Important dates should be tracked—mark them on your desk calendar, put them on your refrigerator, type them into your personal digital assistant (PDA), put them next to the cookie jar—do something. You should also write in important personal dates—birthdays, anniversaries, sports events, scouts or similar activities, and planned vacations. You will need to coordinate your personal schedule with your online class. If you are a parent, gather any and all important events and pencil them in as well. You'll want to avoid as much overlap as possible.

You'll find that in an online class you won't always have a professor who is willing to remind you of upcoming assignments, or who will put reminders on the "chalkboard." This is especially true if you're doing graduate-level course work. The online student is expected to be somewhat independent. There is nothing worse then glancing at your syllabus only to discover that you have a twelve-page paper due in the morning.

Your syllabus is your reminder.

Although not every online learner uses an electronic calendar or PDA, it might be a worthwhile investment to consider. Some online course systems permit you to download the course calendar, announcements, assignments, and even the syllabus to your PDA or online calendar. This is a particularly helpful feature to students who travel or have erratic schedules during a term.

The pace of an online class can be quick, so you will need to keep up every day.

If you can keep a big picture in your mind of what day it is and of upcoming due dates, you can keep track of where you are in the process. Read when you can. Carry reading materials with you. Take notes on your PDA, index cards, scraps of paper—whatever you are using. You can transfer them to the main computer or calendar later.

THE ONLINE DISCUSSION BOARD

Let's continue with the tour. One of the central features of online courses is the discussion board, which enables two or more students to have a conversation at different times. It's often called a *threaded discussion*. One person can post a statement onto an online bulletin board, and a second, third, and fourth person can join the discussion at a later time, and post responses. All members of the group can then read these postings. Over a period of time, we have a threaded discussion. As an online student, you can choose at what point in the conversation you would like to contribute, and your comments could be the third or eighth or even twentieth posting in an extended thread.

As you can imagine, threaded discussions have great potential in the online classroom. In fact, many online instructors rely on the discussion board (see Figure 6.3) as the primary means of communication. This may come as a surprise to those who expected online courses to include a lot of email messages from your professor and classmates. Sure, email is always available, but it's essentially between two individuals. In a face-to-face classroom, if a student has a question, he or she may go up and whisper it into the instructor's ear, but most often he or she asks the question out loud so the entire class can benefit from the answer.

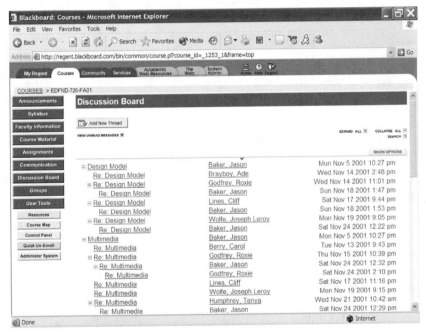

FIGURE 6.3   Sample "Discussion Board."

As a rule, email is for private communication between the instructor and student, or between students themselves, and the threaded discussion is for the class as a whole.

The discussion board and threaded discussion are the most important part of your online experience, in terms of success. In an online classroom, participation equates to presence or *visibility*. Not participating is like not showing up for class. Much of the online instructor's assessment of you and your mastery of course competencies will be based on your public contributions to the class discussions.

You're probably familiar with standard methods used to evaluate students within traditional classes such as quizzes, a midterm, a final exam, a couple of papers, and perhaps attendance or class discussion. Here's where the differences begin with an online course. Online instructors often require students to write papers each week, but more importantly, they require students to contribute regularly to class discussions.

Online students are typically graded on the quality of their critiques of their classmates' work or of their responses to instructor-posted questions.

To do this right, it will require hard work and a commitment of time. For a single course you might need to devote 10 to 15 hours a week—probably in the evenings and on the weekends—doing your assigned reading, writing assignments, and contributing to online discussions. Most students who are working full time will initially find the workload demanding. If you are a procrastinator, and many of us are, you may find yourself up late at night getting those assignments in. And remember, although tests can be given online, most teachers will base their assessments primarily on a student's written work and the quality of their online posts, so allot yourself plenty of time for this important activity.

QUALITY OF ONLINE CONTRIBUTIONS

We once had a professor who had a saying about online posts: "There is a difference between contribution and participation." In order to grade an online activity, such as participation, there must be a measurement. An instructor will often require a minimum number of posts or require posts within a certain period. An online instructor might publish a set of questions related to the week's required reading and then require each student to answer two questions, as well as "replying" to a specified number of their fellow students posts. By reply, we mean they would ask a question of the original author regarding his or her posting, disagree with it, agree with it, or amplify it. The point of these requirements is to encourage an intellectual dialogue. This is the heart of the threaded discussion in an online course.

Students who attempt to meet the weekly posting quota simply by making posts of the ever popular "I agree" or "I couldn't have said it better" are not really con-

tributing to the discussion. They are certainly present and they are participating, but they're not contributing. Do not fall into this trap. Real online contribution takes time and work.

We have devoted quite a bit of discussion to the topic of threaded discussions. That's because it is important.

Contributing—not merely participating—will be your goal throughout the online course.

After you read the announcements and check your email, you'll move onto the discussion boards. This portion of the online course takes discipline. It's best to read the posts of your classmates every day, even if you don't post a contribution. A couple of days of vacation from the discussion board could easily result in fifty to seventy unread messages, even more in a large class. It's important that when you do visit the discussion boards, you actually contribute. This could take several minutes or several hours, depending on the length and depth of your responses, so plan your time accordingly.

Remember that the online instructor will be evaluating your writing to gauge how well you understand the material. You may have to review the weekly readings in preparation for your posts, and that's okay. You will see students in your class who are prolific posters, with their writings comprising twenty-five percent of the class threads, but often not significantly contributing any substance to the discussion.

Quantity is not a substitute for quality.

Take the time to formulate your thoughts carefully, and then draft your responses. Once you respond to someone's thread, look for a follow-up post. When you find yourself in a healthy online debate over some aspect of the subject matter, this is where true learning begins.

There's one other piece of advice that you need to know:

Don't send a posting to a facilitator, professor, classmate, newsgroup, or course discussion board if you are upset or frustrated.

Let the posting sit in the "drafts" folder until you can reread it later. Then, after a day or so, if it reads well, press "send." If not, press the "delete" key and start over. Using this process will most likely save face and prevent hard feelings in the class. Remember, unlike communicating in person where you can always say, "What I meant was . . ." once the send button is pressed online, your message cannot be recalled.

OFFLINE WORK FOR ONLINE SUCCESS

Even when you're taking online courses, much of your online routine will take place offline. You can expect to do a lot of reading in an online course.

Manage your time.

It'll take discipline, and you'll need to find a way to get through the reading while keeping up with the threaded discussions. As we've discussed already, the threaded discussion will be used to gauge your understanding of the material covered in these books. In fact, your instructor will probably draw questions directly from the assigned readings.

You'll also need to give yourself the time to do your writing as well as any group work. Yes, you will probably find yourself in a group project. The challenge, of course, is that your group members will likely be scattered across various states and time zones. This means sending material back and forth around the county via email, and learning to combine your efforts into a group submission. Virtual teams can make for powerful learning experiences, but they take much more time to coordinate than campus groups, so plan accordingly.

One crucial area of offline work that is often overlooked is "taking care of the self." Being an online student and working full time is stressful enough, but if you happen to be married, married with children, or have other responsibilities, you will need to take stock of your time and use it to your advantage.

Know what triggers stress and have a plan for dealing with it. Most often a short walk, putting on some music, or even taking a snack break will help diminish the stress. Don't wait until the night before the assignment is due to catch up with you. You could have server problems or other issues that would keep you from posting the assignment. Some late penalties are pretty steep and you don't want to deal with trying to get things done at the last minute. You will need to be self-directed: here's what I need to do, when I need to do it, and how I need to do it. If you have questions, ask.

SOME FINAL THOUGHTS

This ends the online tour. We hope it was helpful. Just remember that you can be successful in an online course if you manage your time and have the discipline to stick to the schedule. It's very easy to take a few days off because of work or family and then find yourself behind.

Stick to the schedule as much as possible.

Even if you need to take a break because of other commitments, you will want to keep up with the threaded discussion readings—post your responses later in the week when you have time.

Don't let the syllabus get away from you.

Assignments are scheduled weeks in advance and often are designed so that you can start on them before you get through all of the readings.

Don't wait until the last minute.

Rushed work is obvious.

Finally, always contribute.

You will be glad that you did.

Time and Life Management Skills for Online Success

In order to help you anticipate challenges to your online success and to manage your time effectively, reflect on the following questions:

- Realistically, how much time do you have for studying?

  _____

  _____

  _____

- Do you have two to four hours of outside study time per week for each credit of a course?

  _____

  _____

  _____

- When is the best time for you to study—morning, afternoon, or evening?

  _____

  _____

  _____

- How much will you be working? Is this amount of work required or is there some flexibility?

  _____

  _____

  _____

- Have you set aside any time for leisure and social activities?

  _____

  _____

  _____

- How much sleep do you require? Are you getting it?

  _____

  _____

  _____

- Are you eating well? Are you using sugar, salt, and alcohol in moderation?

  _____

  _____

  _____

- Have you set aside time for exercise?

  _____

  _____

  _____

CHAPTER 7

KNOW THYSELF:
TAKING CHARGE OF YOUR
ONLINE LEARNING

MARGARET MARTINEZ

In this chapter, you will learn about:

- Individual learning differences, the impact of self-managing emotions, and intentions for successful learning
- How to change your role as an online student, and develop "take-charge" learning strategies

Over the years, students in the typical classroom setting have been somewhat dependent on the instructor and school for motivation to be in class at a specific time and place, and to get information from the instructor and text. However, for today's online learning requirements, it is no longer enough for a student to rely on instructors and traditional skills learned in the classroom. Successful online students take responsibility and manage their own learning. They develop new strategies that enable them to become more self-directed and self-motivated online students. They are not always taught in the classroom. To acquire online learning skills, they understand individual learning differences and discover how best to learn on their own, whatever the content or situation.

This chapter has two purposes. The first is to discuss individual learning differences, and highlight the impact of self-managing emotions and intentions for more successful learning. The second is to show you how to change your role as a passive learner, and how to develop and practice "take-charge" strategies for more self-motivated, self-directed, independent online learning. The most important strategy is switching your reliance on the instructor to yourself, and over time taking greater responsibility for lifelong learning.

HOW YOU LEARN DIFFERENTLY

Many theories exist today that address how individuals learn differently from one another. A few consider the impact of emotions and intentions, and how these factors influence or guide social and cognitive ability. New developments in the area of brain research are revealing the influence of our brain's emotional center on behavior, learning, and memory. These findings provide us with information about how students learn differently and about possible reasons for these differences. They highlight how emotions—fear, frustration, passion, motivation, and happiness—appear to have a profound impact on learning. In addition, they emphasize how social relationships with the instructor and peers are integral parts of the learning process. Some students depend on these relationships more than others do.

It is natural that, as students, we appreciate instructors who see us as individuals. It makes sense to prefer teachers that identify how we learn differently and support how we each individually learn best. People who tap into our drives, expectations, values, and goals are certainly more likely to get our attention than those who overlook or override our wants and needs.

We respond emotionally.

Yet typical information on how individuals learn differently focuses on a cognitive perspective—how students think or process information differently. But what about how they feel? What about students' preferences on how they best like to learn? Today, a consideration of emotions is important.

By considering the impact of emotions and intentions, instructors can better understand how and why we, as online students, learn differently. For example, some students are happiest learning in collaborative, facilitated environments with learning tasks accomplished in a structured, menu-driven, or linear fashion—one step at a time. Other students may more greatly enjoy email or feedback assistance from a facilitator, who can identify specific steps and schedules towards achievement. Some students thrive in competitive environments that focus on specific details, tasks, and projects, perhaps as a team effort. The more adventurous and independent student may enjoy working in a simulated or action environment, knowing where to find help when necessary.

Additionally, some students need a high degree of structure provided through guidelines, schedules, and rules, particularly if they are learning in an area of low interest. Conversely, other students are passionate about exploring new challenges, making mistakes that discover the unknown, and taking risks. Students who require low maintenance enjoy using learning to achieve their own long-term personal goals, sometimes resisting any kind of learning that appears to have little practical value or benefit.

Students who understand the general impact of emotions and intentions can translate these kinds of emotional and learning differences into individually supportive learning solutions. You can use your own positive emotions to develop personal learning strategies that work best for you, with or without an instructor. The following information provides help for you to identify your important differences, and then develop more personalized learning strategies for greater online learning success.

LEARNING ORIENTATION MODEL

To explore your differences, it is useful to introduce the *learning orientation model*. This model considers the dominant role of emotions and intentions in learning, and how individuals respond differently in various learning situations. Traditional classrooms often rely on instructors to manage the cognitive aspects of learning. In the online learning environment, you need to consider how well you are emotionally prepared to learn independently, with or without an instructor. The learning orientation model discusses three fundamental factors—considered successful learning attributes—that help measure how you may generally want to learn (see Table 7.1).

Self-Motivation

One dictionary defines *conation* as "the part of mental life having to do with striving, including desire and volition." Conative learning attributes estimate your general feelings and attitudes about learning. They describe your will, intent, drive, and degree of passion for learning. They also describe your use of learning as an intrinsic resource to achieve personal goals and satisfy personal needs. These attributes refer to your intentions to learn, influenced to some degree by values, belief, content, people, environments, resources, and

TABLE 7.1. **A Three-Factor Model of Successful Learning Attributes**

FACTOR	DESCRIPTION
Self Motivation	Student's emotional investment in learning, and how the learner uses *internal resources*—passions, intentions, desires, values, and expectations
Strategic Self-Directness	Ability to set, manage, and achieve goals as part of a targeted learning process
Independence (Autonomy)	How much a student uses and relies on *external resources*—instructors, rewards, schedules, rules, and support

instructional presentation. Naturally, successful students are more intentional and apply greater effort in specific courses, topics, or situations that interest or appeal to them.

Strategic Self-Directedness

This attribute describes commitment to your learning and strategic effort. It estimates the degree that you can plan and commit deliberate, strategic effort to accomplish learning. Successful students place great importance on strategic commitment. They enjoy applying focused, strategic, and hard-working principles to learning. Students that appear lower on this factor can be more successful by improving and using key learning strategies (e.g., big picture thinking, self-assessment, reflection, and complex problem solving). Improved long-term planning and increased strategic effort are contributing factors to greater achievement.

Learning Independence or Autonomy

This attribute estimates your desire and ability to take responsibility, make choices, and manage your own learning—independent of the instructor—in the attainment of personal goals. As individuals have different experiences and mature as successful students, they gradually:

- Gain awareness of their learning capabilities and processes, and use this knowledge to improve
- Develop desires for learning control or autonomy
- Assimilate and develop a unique, personal set of learner characteristics
- Commit and self-manage sustained effort to attain personal learning goals
- Review and monitor experiences to improve subsequent learning
- Depend more on internal resources than external resources
- Approach tasks and projects more holistically

THREE LEARNING ORIENTATIONS

The learning orientation model also uses learner attributes to describe three distinct learner types called *learning orientations*. Learning orientations generally discuss how students approach learning differently. The three types are: (1) *transforming*, (2) *performing*, and (3) *conforming*. Most students will typically identify themselves with one orientation, or sometimes with a combination of the learning orientations. Learning orientations are how you choose to learn.

Transforming Learners

Transforming learners use self-directed, strategic planning and holistic thinking to achieve long-term goals. These learners are generally risk-takers, innovators, and highly committed, passionate learners. They most often:

- Place importance on self-managed learning, committed effort, independence, and long-term vision
- Use personal strengths, ability, persistence, challenging strategies, high-standards, learning efficacy, and positive expectations to manage learning successfully
- Lose motivation and become frustrated or resistant in environments that interfere with their assertive learning patterns

To be more successful, these students should focus more on details to ensure task and project completion, and practical application of theories and concepts. Sometimes these students are so intent on exploring the unknown, they forget their original goals and tasks and lose focus. Self-discipline helps them complete one goal or a set of goals before they move on to the next goal. When frustrated, these learners need patience to overcome their limitations and barriers—their strength is the goals that they set for themselves.

Performing Learners

Performing learners are typically more self-directed in areas that they value or that interest them. Otherwise, they may overly rely on external sources for motivation, encouragement, and support. For example, they may intentionally rely on instructors to help them set and manage goals, and accomplish objectives when they do not perceive personal benefit. Typically, these learners are more short-term, project-oriented thinkers who systematically achieve average to above standard learning goals and tasks. They may:

- Enjoy and prefer to focus on concrete details, process, and procedures rather than on abstract concepts and ideas
- Prefer hands-on, competitive, collaborative, or team environments
- May selectively take less responsibility for their learning and rely on external resources for motivation, goal setting, schedules, and direction
- Minimize learning effort by meeting only the stated objectives, or getting the grade, and lose motivation if too much effort is required and rewards are not enough to compensate the perceived effort
- Prefer to learn in classroom, simulated, or interactive environments, especially when they can interact to complete tasks or rely on the instructor to coach them periodically through the achievement process

To be more successful, these learners should consider when and how they tend to rely on an instructor, and reflect on how they are going to make the transition to more self-directed, self-motivated, and independent learning. They can acquire more long-term, holistic thinking skills to find important reasons to motivate and direct themselves towards goal achievement and more challenging efforts. They can learn how to set personal learning goals, and coach themselves through the steps of learning.

Conforming Learners

Conforming learners depend largely on the quality of instruction and support from the environment and social relationships. They prefer to rely on explicit guidance and simple steps provided by an instructor. Complex online learning environments may frustrate them with too many opportunities to make mistakes. These learners are concerned with safety, security, and acceptance. Conforming learners generally:

- Prefer progress in a step-by-step fashion
- Are good at repetitive tasks and consistent expectations
- Are less confident learners
- React strongly to external influences
- Prefer supportive, structured environments
- Have less desire to take risks, to control or manage their learning, and to initiate change in their jobs or environment
- Are challenged in open learning environments that focus on discovery or exploratory learning

Typically, these students want to learn in classrooms where they can find a concerned instructor who can be supportive, and guide them through the learning process. To be more successful, these learners can acquire and depend on more risk-taking, problem solving, holistic thinking skills to find reasons and ways to motivate and direct themselves towards more challenging efforts. They can understand how they learn best and choose opportunities that fit their requirements. These learners can strive to achieve greater independence that enables them to trust themselves and take greater responsibility for their own learning over time. Nevertheless, they can ask for help, as they need it.

PERSONALIZING YOUR ONLINE
LEARNING ENVIRONMENT

Your challenge, as today's online student, is to identify which elements of online learning provide the best results for your personal learning needs. The task is two-fold. First, you need to consider the type of learning environment that works best for you—with or without an instructor or facilitator. Second, you need to determine what type of instructional presentation best matches and supports your interests, values, and learning expectations, including what level of social interaction best matches those interests, values, and expectations. Then, you can better judge your online learning ability and requirements, determine gaps between how you like to learn and the typical online learning situation, and identify strategies for your long-term online learning and performance improvement.

TABLE 7.2   **Description of Personalized Learning Environments**

LEARNING ORIENTATIONS	PERSONALIZED LEARNING ENVIRONMENTS
Transforming Learners	• Sophisticated and discovery-oriented • Loosely structured & flexible environments • Challenging goals • Holistic planning strategies • Complex concepts • Problem solving • Self-managed learning • Adaptive environments that allow learner to be assertive • Ability to control, self-direct, and self-assess
Performing Learners	• Semi-structured and hands-on environments • Stimulate personal values and encourage teamwork • Provide details, tasks, processes, procedures, and project completion • Task-oriented, energizing, and competitive • Provide practice and feedback to encourage self-motivation, problem solving, self-monitoring, and task sequencing • Minimizes the need for extra effort and difficult standards
Conforming Learners	• Safe, low-learner controlled, structured environments • Help learners achieve comfortable, low-risk learning goals in a linear fashion • Explicit, careful guidance and collaborative learning tools • Help learners in a step-by-step fashion • Pace supportive and enjoyable

Personalized Learning Environments

The first step in improving your online learning ability is to consider the learning environment that works best for you—with or without an instructor or facilitator. A closely matched learning environment will have a positive impact on your learning. Table 7.2 identifies what type of environment best matches how you prefer to learn.

Identifying Learning Strategies for Various Instructional Situations

The second step in improving online learning ability is to consider the presentation of instruction and interaction that work best for you. The three factors that can strongly influence how you can improve learning involve increased *self-motivation, self-direction, and learning autonomy*. To identify your best online learning strategies, review the strategies in Table 7.3 in order to consider how they can enhance your current online learning ability. These strategies also describe potential strengths and weaknesses, and enable learners to grow.

CONCLUSION

The goal of this chapter is to help you think about how to achieve more self-motivated, self-directed, and independent learning in the online environment. This chapter can expand your understanding about your own learning orientation. In order to improve your online learning ability, you need to consider the often overlooked impact of emotions and intentions on learning, and how design and presentation strategies for learning environments and instruction can also powerfully influence how you *want to learn, how you intend to learn, and how you actually do learn online*.

If you want to achieve greater online learning success, you need to take greater responsibility for your own learning strategies, rather than depending too much on others.

TABLE 7.3 Description of Different Instructional Strategies

LEARNING STRATEGIES	TRANSFORMING LEARNERS	PERFORMING LEARNERS	CONFORMING LEARNERS
SELF-MOTIVATION			
General Learning Situation	• High-learner controlled • Open learning situation • High stimulation, exploration, and problem solving • Occasional mentoring and interaction • Discovery	• Competitive, hands-on learning situation • Medium stimulation and processing capacity • Consistent coaching and interaction • Collaborative	• Consistent and simple learning situation • Minimal stimulation and processing capacity • Continual, explicit guidance and reinforcement • Trust-building
Feedback	• Praise and recognition by mentors	• Praise and recognition by peers	• Praise and recognition by peers for incremental achievement
Rewards and Recognition	• Continual opportunity for innovation and improvement	• Competitive or team reward structures • Continuing opportunity for increasing expertise and project completion	• Opportunities to apply and reinforce newly acquired expertise
Type of Information	• Holistic, theoretical information to solve long-term problems and achieve personal goals • Enhance information gathering with increasing specifics and practical application	• Practical, specific information to solve short-term problems, complete projects, and demonstrate expertise • Enhance information gathering with increasing holistic or conceptual information	• Simple, guided information to solve short-term problems, complete assignments, and show accomplishments • Enhance information gathering with increasing levels of problem solving

(continued)

TABLE 7.3 (*Continued*)

LEARNING STRATEGIES	TRANSFORMING LEARNERS	PERFORMING LEARNERS	CONFORMING LEARNERS
Content Structuring	• Freedom to construct content • Opportunities for new knowledge and innovation	• Freedom to accomplish tasks and projects with minimal effort	• Freedom to rely on help from others to guide content structure, progress, and outcomes
Quality of Interaction	• High-standards environment with sophisticated goals and challenging accomplishment • Frustrated by too much focus on detail, short-term goals, and lack of long-term accomplishment	• Competitive, interactive environment focused on project completion and increased expertise • Frustrated by extra time and effort required for slow peer interaction, long-term goals, or unmet needs	• Guided participatory environment with directions provided by instructor • Frustrated by fast pace, complex processes, and high-level standards
LEARNING AUTONOMY			
Independence	• Assumes learning responsibility independent of the instructor • Frustration if placed in restricted environments with limited learner control	• Assumes learning responsibility in areas of keen interest • Frustrated if topics are of less interest or if in restrictive environment	• Assumes learning responsibilities to make own decisions about learning • Use structured environments to acquire self-directed learning skills • Frustrated if denied responsibility for learning

Relationship to Instructors	• Resources to expand knowledge-building opportunities and attainment of long-term personal goals	• Coaches • Interaction with peers as added resource to enhance expertise and project completion	• Guidance from instructors • Careful interaction with peers as added resource to increase achievement of low-risk goals
SELF-DIRECTION			
Goal-Setting	• Challenging goals • Maximize effort to attain increasingly difficult standards beyond those set by others	• Average to high standards • Negotiate standards and consider long-term goals	• Simple, task-oriented goals • Take incremental steps and increase effort in supportive environments with safe, manageable standards
Task Sequencing	• According to performance needs, personal learning requirements, holistic information expectations and varying levels of expertise • Consider influences on intrinsic values and benefits	• According to interactive performance needs, detailed information needs and increasing levels of expertise • Consider influences on external values and benefits	• According to manageable steps, low-risk performance requirements, and less complex, safety-based information needs • Consider influences on stability and conformance
Knowledge Building	• Discover and build new knowledge • Consider practical application of new knowledge	• Assimilate and apply relevant knowledge • Develop interest in exploring related issues and discovering long-term results	• Accept and reproduce knowledge to meet external requirements • Develop trust in assimilating and experimenting with application of new knowledge

(continued)

TABLE 7.3 (*Continued*)

LEARNING STRATEGIES	TRANSFORMING LEARNERS	PERFORMING LEARNERS	CONFORMING LEARNERS
Problem Solving	• Complex, holistic, problem-solving opportunities that lead to new content or knowledge • Consider part-to-whole solutions and practical applications	• Competitive part-to-whole problem solving for specific projects and tasks • Develop trust in conceptual ability and long-term thinking	• Simple problem-solving opportunities that reconfirm achievement and acceptance • Work with guide to develop trust in own learning and problem solving ability
Practice	• Apply knowledge toward project completion	• Consider conceptual knowledge and long-term implications	• Consider related and increasingly difficult problems
Assessment	• Self-assess achievements based on challenging standards and long-term personal goals	• Self-assess and seek assessment from others • Review achievements based on short-term goals and negotiated standards	• Seek assessment from others • Consider accomplishments based on short-term goals and standards aligned with group
Questioning	• To expand knowledge and to apply new knowledge • To consider practical details	• To solve problems and complete projects • To seek opportunities to understand related concepts and long-term consequences	• To accomplish assignments • To seek opportunities to understand related concepts and long-term consequences

APPLICATION EXERCISE 7A

What Kind of Learner Are You?

Based on your reading of this chapter, are you a *transforming, performing,* or *conforming* learner? What are your characteristics as this kind of online learner and what skills will you require?

CHARACTERISTICS	SKILLS REQUIRED

Taking Charge of Your Learning

In order to develop your skills as an online student, list the top ten "take charge" learning strategies or things you must do in order to remind yourself to emphasize your existing skills and to develop new attitudes and skills.

1. _____
   _____

2. _____
   _____

3. _____
   _____

4. _____
   _____

5. _____
   _____

6. _____
   _____

7. _____
   _____

8. _____
   _____

9. _____
   _____

10. _____
    _____

CHAPTER 8

THE ONLINE INSTRUCTOR'S POINT OF VIEW

JUDY DONOVAN

In this chapter, you will learn about:

- Insights from the online instructor's perspective
- How online learners can improve their educational experience

This chapter explains an instructor's point of view to you—the new or experienced online student—so that you may have a more successful experience. Much of what is contained in this chapter can also apply to traditional face-to-face classes, but most matter more in the online classroom.

A DAY IN THE LIFE OF THE ONLINE INSTRUCTOR

Online instructors vary in their daily activities. Some are full-time academics with a teaching load comprising traditional and online classes, and with the usual demands in their schedules for research, publication, meetings, and various other duties. Many have careers outside of academia in business or industry, and teach a class or two on the side. Some may work part time and teach part time, while others may combine consulting and instructing.

Your online instructor is most likely a busy professional with responsibilities well beyond teaching the class you are taking. This does not mean you deserve less attention. But it's a good bet that your instructor is an adjunct or part-time instructor, otherwise employed in business or industry. In fact, some online colleges only hire active professionals to teach—they feel the real life, current experience such a person has to offer is invaluable to students. As an online student, you probably also work full time and have other responsibilities such as a family. So you probably will be able to relate to your instructor.

A typical day for adjunct online instructors is to rise, eat, and check email or the classroom for urgent messages. They might typically work 9 to 5 or longer, so they might check the classroom messages and email at lunch as well. Then they arrive home, or to their hotel if traveling, and log into the classroom again. They must read all the posts, responding to some and monitoring the discussion, answer questions, respond to email, make sure lectures and assignments are posted, perhaps grade an assignment and—whew, before you know it—it's time for bed.

In an accelerated class that is 4–8 weeks long, online teaching can be very labor intensive. There may be three to five assignments per week, times 10–15 students to grade, plus daily email, questions, all the hundreds of postings per week to read and respond to, student problems and emergencies to handle, and more. An online instructor is challenged to get into all the discussions and interact as much as possible with the students—and meet all the administrative work and grading requirements called for.

Weekends are generally the time to catch up—do grade reports, email students who are inactive or missing assignments, and attempt to get on top of things. If there are papers due that week, the only time to grade them may be the weekends. I set aside Saturday mornings to grade an average of 15 papers. I dig out the description of the assignment including criteria such as length, subject, and style. I locate the assignments wherever they are posted and download and open each one. I scan all of the papers first and then grade each one individually, correcting mechanics, grammar, misspellings, style, content, and organization. I offer detailed comments and feedback. I then email each one back to the student and record the grades. That takes care of my Saturday mornings. No problem . . . if everything goes smoothly. But what about the papers I can't open because they are saved in some obscure word processor? Or the ones posted to the wrong place I have to hunt down? Or the ones with so many errors I spend an hour just correcting mechanics. Or the late ones not available Saturday morning? I may have to make time to go through the entire process again.

Given all that, why do instructors accept the challenges and responsibilities to teach online? Well, there are a number of good reasons. Many instructors teach online because it offers a consistent and interesting connection to other people. Some enjoy the interaction and multinational, varied students involved in online classes. Although the money may not be great—adjuncts get paid approximately $1000 to $1800 for a six-week class; $2000 to $2800 for a semester-long class—it can be good supplemental income. For many working professionals, though, online teaching is a way to share our experiences. I love it when a student asks for my input. This gives me a chance to share information that goes beyond the textbook. Keep in mind, as a professional in the field, I find the textbook is a starting point for talking about my own experiences. That is very rewarding.

So what's the point? Like you, online instructors are busy. One survey I read showed that one-third of online instructors spend 11–15 hours per week per class, and over half spend more than 16 hours per week per class teaching and preparing. It is a lot more hours if this is the first time the instructor is teaching the class, and he or she is preparing materials, lectures, and handouts while teaching.

The more you are aware of these issues and understand your instructor, the more you can do your part to make the class a great experience for all involved.

MAKING A GOOD FIRST IMPRESSION

As a new online student, you most likely want to get off on the right foot in your classroom—first impressions are important. This desire may be challenged when problems arise right from the beginning. For example, you might not be able to be online for a few days, or through no fault of your own, you lack the textbook.

Explain the problem to the instructor in an email, and assure him or her of your responsibility. The instructor might even be able to help.

Take the time to carefully read the syllabus and other introductory materials. You would be surprised how many students neglect this elementary step. Much of what you need to know is found in these materials. Online instructors know who hasn't read them by their posts—do they ask questions that are answered in the syllabus or the first lecture? Are they posting assignments in the wrong place or on the wrong day? It is important to find out what the instructor wants you to do.

Take the time to read the course materials provided for you. It will save you and your instructor time and effort.

Generally, the first assignment will be a "get-to-know-each-other" type that involves telling about you, and reading what the other students and the instructor have posted about themselves. Instructors may want you to use a student page, if the software provides this. Others want a brief posting to the chat room or some other designated area. Many instructors ask that you address specific points in this posting. For example, I ask students to let me know their time zones as I form learning groups based on geographic proximity.

When you know what you are supposed to do, then you can do it well. Put forth special effort. Post personal details about yourself, such as hobbies, where you live, and interests so that other students and the instructor can begin to form a picture of you. Read all of the other students' and the instructor's postings and respond to specifics you can relate to. Many online students rush through the introductory activities. This can create an impression of someone who is disorganized, is too busy to participate, or doesn't care.

Make sure you check out all messages, however briefly, to get to know the instructor and other students in your class, and to be aware of any changes that have been made.

It is best to avoid emailing the instructor during the first few days of class or before class starts. Instead, use this time to read over the course materials carefully and give yourself a chance to answer your own questions first. If you do have a question about the first assignment, post it to the classroom, or to an area designated for questions. It is less likely to get lost in the email deluge, and another online student may have the answer. Make sure you label your question in the subject line of your message so the instructor can easily spot it.

The early assignments you submit in class are part of the instructor's first impression of your academic abilities. They may be a response to a discussion question, a short paper, or answers to textbook questions. Whatever the assignment, take the time to do a thorough job. Answer all parts of the question; put in sufficient detail or personal experience to clarify your answers. Watch your spelling, and post on time. Take a few minutes to comment on your classmates' answers.

Some instructors don't mind if you post an assignment a day or two early. Others think it interferes with the discussion flow and may inhibit other students' creativity. If this issue is not covered in the syllabus, you may want to post a question to get clarification. If you are unable to post the assignment on the day it is due and the instructor discourages early assignment posting, then contact the instructor for advice.

In the first week of the online class, make sure you understand the requirements for participation. This should be in the syllabus. In addition, get an idea of when and how to expect feedback. Does the instructor use an online gradebook? Are grades sent once a week after the week has finished? If the syllabus does not address these issues, you may just need to wait and see. I would not advise posting questions or emailing the instructor about grading and feedback issues the first week—give him or her a chance to show you how things are done. Be patient.

In addition, when you send a paper to the instructor, don't ask for confirmation that it is received. This makes unnecessary busywork for the instructor.

Assume it has been received unless you hear otherwise. You might have a return receipt feature on your email, or you can look at sent mail to show that you did submit the assignment on time should it become an issue.

The last area to address in this first week is your online tone. Make sure you are courteous and show respect in your online postings. Ask a question to clarify if you don't understand someone's point. Disagree gently—qualify your comments with words like, "In my experience . . ." or "This article I found seems to say . . ." Some instructors and students like to play devil's advocate to get discussion going. This is great. Just keep it friendly. Don't expect everyone to agree with you. There are a lot of points of view represented in the classroom.

In summary, to make a good first impression in your online class, pay attention to the tone, content, and mechanics of your assignments and postings. Begin the class right by doing a good job with the introductory activities. Make sure you have read the course materials, know what to do, and interact with your classmates.

THE *DO*s OF ONLINE LEARNING

I wanted to get many instructors' points of view to include in this chapter, so I posted questions in an informal survey to listservs and online college faculty bulletin boards. I also emailed the entire faculty at one online college. Over fifty online instructors responded, and what struck me was how similar their answers were. There does seem to be general agreement in what instructors appreciate and don't appreciate in their students.

The first question I asked was "How should students go about establishing a good instructor/student relationship with you?" Many instructors mentioned the points covered above: read the syllabus, understand the course software, make sure you have your textbook and other materials, and make sure your email is working. In addition, they mentioned things such as "communicate, put forth a good effort, show an interest in the course and in your fellow students, ask questions if you don't understand something, and be courteous." Additional comments included:

- "If students communicate effectively and efficiently, our relationship will always be positive, and I will be as flexible as possible in working with them."
- "I think one of the best ways to establish a good relationship is for students to start the class with a positive attitude, especially toward their peers. If students are respectful of each other, it helps the student/instructor relationship. I also think they should be willing to be open and responsive in their postings."
- "Students obviously glean instructors' favor by being dedicated, hard working, and willing to go the extra mile to learn."
- "Demonstrate they are interested in the learning process by responding promptly to the assignments and introducing themselves to the learning community."
- "They can establish a good relationship with me by taking responsibility for their education and being accountable for their course work."
- "It helps if the student is friendly."
- "By making it apparent they have done their homework, by submitting well-written messages, and by following the guidelines established in the course syllabus."

- "Online I find that the relationships the students establish with each other in the discussion threads is a way for them to show me that they care and are enjoying the class. Their enthusiasm for the class goes a long way in establishing a relationship with me as an instructor."
- "I appreciate those that help their peers. I try to formulate a team in class so we're there for each other. Some students never buy into this and will neither answer or ask questions with anyone but me."
- "By taking the responsibility to accept the fact that they must discipline and organize their life to meet the rigors of an online class, establishes a favorable rapport with me."

THE *DON'Ts* OF ONLINE LEARNING

I also asked online instructors for their pet peeves regarding online students. As with what instructors appreciate, the things they don't appreciate are quite specific. They include:

- Not reading syllabus, instructor messages, email, course materials, questions already addressed
- Late work and not following directions
- Causing a lot of off-topic discussion or one-line replies such as "I agree"
- Negative comments on discussion boards and rudeness
- Email with no name or course number (who is *lucky49@hotmail.com?*)
- Students who don't participate
- Not correcting work after feedback

Other responses to the question "What are your pet peeves when it comes to students?" were:

- "Complaining about the workload after they chose to complete their degree in an accelerated online program."
- "Not learning the platform. I have one student who didn't bother to go through the tutorial. I am constantly receiving emails that read, "I don't mean to bother you, and I hope I am not a pest, but how do I . . .?"
- "What bothers me most are those who *constantly* miss deadlines because of work related-incidents, family incidents, taking vacations in the middle of a session, or trying to enter late because they thought that the class started on a different date."
- "Students who do not contribute or communicate with me regarding assignments, etc. If I do not hear from students as requested, I become less flexible. If they communicate with me, I can be as flexible as possible."

- "Students who acknowledge that my time is valuable immediately win my favor; those who assume I should be online 24/7 to answer their questions are off to a poor start."
- "One of the biggest concerns I have is with group work . . . that is, when a student does not carry his or her load."
- "My biggest peeve centers around students who try to scam me, saying they had sent in an assignment and when I say I didn't receive it, they say they'll resend it right away. When I check the file properties I find it had been created the night before."
- "Do not conduct personal attacks on other students."

The main concern of online instructors is communication.

The online syllabus, assignment descriptions, lectures, and postings are all forms of communication that contain clear instructions for how work is to be completed, by what due date, and where to submit it. Ignoring this information can be time consuming for you and the instructor.

You may feel instructors are being contradictory when we say we appreciate students who ask questions, but then list students as pet peeves who post questions that are already answered in the course materials. You have read in this book about student responsibility and how it is important to the online classroom. This translates to making an effort to find the answer rather than posting a question to the class or emailing the instructor. In addition, don't be a student whose work is chronically late for one reason or another. If you are constantly in a state of emergency, perhaps you need to get your life in order before you take classes. Make sure your problems don't impact the instructor or the class.

Finally, plagiarism can be a real problem for the instructor in the online world. A few years ago, a quarter or more of my students turned in papers that contained plagiarism. The most common form of plagiarism is copy and paste. Students copy entire paragraphs or sentences from their sources and paste them into their paper. They might stick the source at the end, but they don't use quotes to indicate that someone else wrote the section. I have received five-page papers composed entirely of these types of paragraphs. Through experience, I have honed the Academic Honesty section in my syllabus so that it is crystal clear.

You can never use someone else's words without quotes. Ignorance is not an excuse.

DON'T BE ONE OF THESE ONLINE STUDENTS

Susan Ko and Steve Rossen, in their *Teaching Online: A Practical Guide* (New York: Houghton Mifflin, 2001), discuss several types of students who can present particular problems for instructors.

Noisy Students

"A noisy student in an online classroom, much like his or her traditional counterpart, spends much energy raising issues that are only tangentially related to the topics under discussion. One way this occurs online is that the student will begin new topic threads even when the comments he or she has to contribute actually fit in with existing threads. Such students often avoid replying to anything but the instructor's comments. And when they do join in the discussion, they generally ignore the direction of the conversation and simply pepper the thread with inane comments."

Must-Have-an-A Students

These are rare, but some students will email the instructor to inform them that they have a 4.0 average and they sure hope this class won't ruin it. Or, in an introductory email, they say they have to pass the class. Remember that you will be judged by what you do in the class, not by anything else. One instructor said, "The grade monger is worried only about maintaining a 4.0 and not about learning the material. Closely in second place is the student who thinks it is my fault they are going to lose their 4.0 average as a result of this class."

Know-It-All Students

No one likes to be contradicted—not instructors and not other students. Find a way to contribute and accept other points of view at the same time.

Complainers

Complaints about the assignments, the workload, the instructor, the textbook, everything, are not productive. If you give specifics, perhaps your complaints can be rectified. But complaining about everything results in the complaints becoming the focus.

Quiet Students

These online students don't participate. No one knows if you are "lurking," reading everything but not posting. But no one cares either—you are graded on what you contribute. *You need to be visible.*

Rude Students

Some students use inappropriate tone or language. They seem to feel they are in an anonymous chat room and can say whatever they want. Common courtesy is a must.

Anxious Students

Don't email the instructor every day asking about grades and arguing about every little point deduction. Don't call the instructor at home with every little problem. Show some patience and confidence in yourself.

CONCLUSION

Instructors vary in their experience, training, enthusiasm, time commitments, and more. The same instructor can teach the same class and have two very different experiences. A lot of what happens depends upon you and the other students in the online class. This chapter gave you some ideas about what instructors appreciate in their online students, and how to form a positive relationship with your online instructor.

Do your job as an online student—work hard, learn, and follow instructions. And as a person, if you are polite and positive, you will do great!

HELPFUL RESOURCES

http://www.onenw.org/bin/page.cfm?pageid=29
http://www.techsoup.org/articlepage.cfm?ArticleId=118&topicid=5

Insights from Online Instructors

List the most important insights you received from this chapter:

1. _____

   _____

   _____

   _____

2. _____

   _____

   _____

   _____

3. _____

   _____

   _____

   _____

4. _____

   _____

   _____

   _____

5. _____

   _____

   _____

   _____

■ ■ ■ ■ ■ ▬▬▬▬▬▬▬▬▬▬▬▬▬▬▬▬

CHAPTER 9

TIPS FOR ONLINE READING, WRITING, AND DISCUSSING

CAROLYN GALE

In this chapter, you will learn about:

- Issues related to reading and writing volumes of messages and assignments, using email, and an online discussion system
- Hints to help you adjust and thrive in an online text-based environment

Unlike a face-to-face class, online courses operate mostly in the world of text. You'll encounter numerous pages of articles and messages to read, and plenty of messages and assignments of your own to write. These assignments, messages, and discussions are the heart of an online course, so it is very important to consider some of the major issues when working in the universe of text. These issues include how to adjust to the amount of writing and typing, how often to contribute messages and responses, and how much to write in a message. In the following chapter, I will offer tips or suggestions with some supportive anecdotes. My hope is that you will learn from the online experiences that I have encountered and improve your online reading, writing, and discussing.

KEEP YOUR ONLINE INSTRUCTOR INFORMED

As many online educators and students have observed, the online classroom can be a cold medium. Unlike face-to-face communication, students receive no instant feedback to their questions or comments. They don't immediately know how people respond to their ideas. Such silence can feel isolating and unnerving, not warm and supportive. As an online student, you may not be a good typist and therefore won't be able to churn out lots of discussion comments quickly. This can challenge your time, skills, and motivation.

After taking one online course, I found that a text-based learning environment does not necessarily have to be cold. The more I interacted with my online instructor about my concerns and needs, the more I felt closer to him as a human being. And I found that there are real advantages to a text-based medium. For example, I enjoyed having a text archive of all of the work the class completed over the semester. I could review past comments carefully and respond more fully. My discussion comments became more thoughtful. The entire experience became incredibly rewarding.

Consequently, although you may begin an online course disliking the text-based environment, you will finish the course a better communicator. Although many of us may prefer communicating orally and face to face, a good online course shows us how it is possible to communicate with only text and even to make it enjoyable.

If, at the start of the course, you alert your online instructor to the kind of help you need, you'll be less likely to lose confidence in your skills, to decrease your intrinsic motivation, and most drastically, to drop out. Most importantly, you will more likely enjoy your experience.

NEVER UNDERESTIMATE HOW MUCH YOU WILL WRITE

Everything that you would normally just say out loud in a traditional class has to be written and submitted in an online class. Words add up quickly. In my first online classes, I found myself drowning in text overload. Even with as few as nine students, sometimes I would find 50–100 backlogged messages—many 4–6 pages long—just because I had taken a day or two off from reading email or logging in to a conferencing system.

Not only will you be writing assignments to be submitted to your instructor for review, you will likely be interacting with your peers through written messages. This requires logging in to a conferencing system to read numerous written messages, as well as composing your own responses. Sometimes you will have group work to complete, and online this means writing and posting personal emails.

In other words, be prepared to spend a lot of time at your keyboard during the time you take your course. You might even consider taking a keyboarding class prior to your course if your typing skills are a bit rusty or lacking.

In addition, good writing always involves a lot of rewriting. If you believe that you should write perfect assignments the first time around, you may be setting yourself up for frustration. You will have to outline, write drafts, edit, and rewrite. For example, before you start writing, always leave time to outline what you will say, and the order you will say it. Leave time at the end to proofread for spelling, grammar, and meaning.

Plan to rewrite, rewrite, and rewrite.

LOGON AS OFTEN AS POSSIBLE

I found that if I didn't make a habit of logging on at least once a day, I would fall behind in the reading and processing of numerous messages. Like you, I had other things competing for my time. If I didn't schedule my time carefully, I'd find myself frantically logging on the day of a deadline to finish an assignment.

If you don't make the time to logon often, be prepared for a shock when you have a large backlog of messages.

I think you'll find that the "anytime, anywhere" asynchronous learning of the online classroom can be a double-edged sword. For example, if you run into some family problems that require a significant amount of time on top of your regular work and school schedule, you may find that you do not have enough time to work on your online assignments.

Communicate with your online instructor immediately.

If you do not have any release time to complete your course, you may end up doing marathon weekends and evenings to complete the work. Try to set up a schedule that can anticipate and adjust to these kinds of situations. Always talk your way through them with your online instructor.

Getting into the habit of logging on daily and communicating with your instructor will have a ripple effect when the course is in full swing, and will decrease the chance of falling behind.

As previously discussed in this handbook, online interaction requires a different approach than face-to-face interaction. Whether you are communicating through email, through a discussion in a bulletin board type newsgroup, or through a more informal chat room, there are a number of guidelines used in the online classroom. Review Chapter 5, "Communicating in the Online Classroom," or access rules by a group called Responsible Use of the Network at *http://www.dtcc.edu/cs/rfc1855.html.*

DO YOUR OWN ASSIGNMENT BEFORE
READING ANOTHER'S

One online course that I took had a conferencing system with an interesting twist. With some assignments, a student would have to post an assignment first before being able to view the others. This can be done with "write-only" meetings or newsgroups, where students only send messages, not read the messages of others. The policy allowed students to post their thoughts and concerns without everyone focusing on the message of the first person to post. I found this rather valuable. Even if I posted the same idea or opinion as someone else, it would be in my own words. This is much better and more substantial involvement than simply saying, "Oh, that's what I thought," or "Yep, I agree with everyone here." You'll feel less intimidated, and you will probably have a different point of view than other students' responses.

If your conferencing system does not have this feature, I suggest that you read the assignment, ignore the responses of others, and think about what your answer would be first. Write your own response and post it. This can be intimidating, but try not to worry about what others are planning for their assignments. If you are hesitant to be the first to post a response, keep your answers "offline" on your computer until others have posted their work. But don't peek if you can help it!

BE VISIBLE AND COMMUNICATE OFTEN

Unlike a face-to-face class, it will be obvious to your instructor and other students if you do not participate. You must be visible. Simply logging in daily and reading messages is important, but not enough. Obviously, when an assignment is due, you need to write something and submit it. However, there is more here than meets the eye. You should go the extra mile. Get to know the other online students. Begin by introducing yourself to your classmates and responding to the introductions of others with enthusiastic and "chatty" messages. This attitude spreads to all online assignments and throughout the course.

Make sure that you read other students' responses—reflect on those messages, and respond with thoughtful, relevant, and enthusiastic comments.

During one online course I took, the "cybercafe" or "chat" meeting place was very quiet. We had all introduced ourselves and that seemed to be the end of it. During one day, though, I decided to submit a controversial editorial I had written about using computers in the classroom—a "lightning rod" to spark discussion. Did it ever! Everyone had an opinion and the conversation went on for a week. That was the icebreaker that kept all of us "talking" away for the rest of the semester. At the end of the course, the instructor told me that my article had really stirred up the class, and she was very grateful for that post.

Another opportunity to be visible and communicate is when another classmate "falls behind" in his or her work and submits postings late. In one course I took, a classmate sent in a posting three weeks late. Since we all wanted this student to feel that she was still part of the online class, we went back to the prior assignments and provided feedback and continued our past conversation. Our instructor was grateful for this communication and pointed out that past assignments and conversations are never really closed.

DON'T "LURK"

A "lurker" is someone who never posts messages to a conferencing system or newsgroup, but is taking the class, completing assignments, and reading the messages of others in the online conversation. You can think of this person as the one who sits quietly in the rear of a traditional classroom, and who never asks questions in class or participates in a discussion. Usually, a lurker is someone who is shy or intimidated by the medium, or highly pressed for time in other aspects of life. In any case, this is a lose-lose situation. The class loses valuable input and a richer sense of community.

The lurker misses out on personal opportunities for growth and connections that could have been gained by more wholly participating in the course.

If you are feeling intimidated at any point in the course, again contact your instructor. Try to be specific about what you feel the "problem" is. Perhaps a classmate wrote something offensive, or you are feeling intimidated by the level of expertise that other classmates have. In any case, try to pinpoint what makes you feel uncomfortable. This will help your instructor in terms of responding to the issue.

If you don't have time to post anything for an extended time, it is a courtesy to your classmates to let them know. Of course, you should have already notified your instructor. A short message of explanation is sufficient.

By the way, if you are taking a course for credit, you will have no choice but to participate in class. It's part of your grade. However, if you are auditing a class—not taking for credit—and are hesitant to "dive in," ask your instructor if you can participate, and what would be required of you. Even if you are auditing an online course, you should be visible, just like the auditor sitting in on a traditional class.

THINK QUALITY AS WELL AS QUANTITY

Although being visible in the online class and contributing a number of messages are key to succeeding in the online classroom, the quality of your postings and responses is also important. In terms of responding to another online student, simply writing, "I agree with everything you say" or "Good job!" is not enough. If you agree with a message, include a couple sentences of explanation. Be specific. Your response should tell the reader what idea or point you agree with. You should start by quoting the specific sentence or paragraph that you wish to address, and then add your response. The same goes for disagreements as well, but try to be as courteous as possible.

Keep in mind that your online instructor and classmates probably won't relish the idea of printing out pages of explanation, much less trying to read a large amount of information on a screen.

If you are responding to several interesting ideas, break your responses up into separate messages. You'll have a better chance of being read and encouraging someone to respond.

Being thoughtful in your responses can take more time, but remember that other classmates won't have time to decipher vague messages or read long postings. Neither will you!

SHOW RESPECT FOR OTHERS' WORK

Sometimes, you'll find yourself disagreeing—perhaps strongly—about something an online peer or instructor wrote. It's very important to avoid "flaming" in an email or conferencing system, or writing anything that could be construed as offensive. If someone has offended you, be careful not to post a strong response right away. Wait 24 hours and see how you feel about the message then. Your intent might not be offensive, but we lose the nuances of body language and intonation found in a face-to-face class.

Effective online communication takes the perception and possible interpretations of the receiver into consideration.

If you wish to disagree with someone's work, do your best to say something positive at the start of your response. Of course, be truthful, but you can almost always find something to agree with in the other person's statement. Try to be as specific as possible about the issue you are concerned with, and use "I statements" as much as possible in your response. For example, try writing, "I am confused by your message and would appreciate some clarification on topic X," instead of "Your message makes no sense at all."

It might be helpful to run your response by someone else first—even your instructor. In fact, if any problems occur, I strongly suggest contacting your instructor *before* communicating with a classmate personally. It is easier over private email for issues to become more attacking in nature.

Remember, starting a "flame war" online—whether public or private—will lower class morale and make it difficult for others as well as you to have a positive experience.

KEEP YOUR MESSAGES FOCUSED

What happens if you want to respond to a very long message? I suggest responding to one idea at a time. When you hit "reply," remove all portions of the original message that don't pertain to your response. That way, others won't share in the overload, and your response will more likely be read.

In other words, be concise without being overly terse. When replying to a message, include enough of the original material to be understood but that's it. It is extremely bad taste to reply to a message by including the entire previous message. You often force readers to go through all sorts of irrelevant information to get to your point. Done often enough, it gets extremely frustrating.

Edit out all the irrelevant material.

Another idea is to be aware that you are replying to a specific message. Discussion systems that show the hierarchy of responses are helpful in determining to whom you are responding or to what portion of a message you are responding. Taking some time at the start of the course to understand how your particular system works will help keep your responses, and responses to your work, easy to find.

Be sure to utilize all areas of your conferencing system—sometimes a post would be more appropriate in a "chat" section than within the regular meeting world of weekly assignments. Don't hesitate to contact your instructor if you feel that there should be a new topic area or "thread" created for students to post more appropriately.

CONCLUSION

As this chapter has shown, there are many things you can do to adjust to the text-based environment of an online course. Among them:

- Check in often or be prepared for information overload.
- Respond to postings and show respect for others' work.
- Keep your postings short and make it easy for someone to respond.
- Contact your instructor if you become intimidated, offended, or behind.
- Avoid "lurking."
- Expect to write and rewrite.
- Show respect for others online and follow online "netiquette."
- Keep your messages clear and focused.

Best of luck as you navigate through the world of text!

APPLICATION EXERCISE 9A

Improving Visibility by Clarifying Online Comments

If you want to improve visibility in the online class, one way of doing that is to clarify comments in discussion. But that can be a challenge—what do you say? How do you respond to other people's comments? You can improve visibility and generate comments by asking questions for clarification. Four important areas interfere with online students understanding one another: (1) leaving words out, (2) vague pronouns, (3) vague verbs, and (4) vague nouns.

Leaving words out of online sentences and discussions leaves readers not knowing exactly what the writer means. You can deal with left-out words by asking for the information that is missing. Following are statements that leave out words or have vague pronouns, verbs, and nouns, and examples of questions you can use online to clarify them.

STATEMENTS	QUESTIONS
I don't understand.	About what? About whom?
I agree.	What you agree with?
It's incredible.	What is incredible?
They say ethics is situational.	Who says?
My parents pushed me to enter business.	What did they do to push you?
I love the lecture.	Specifically, what was it about the lecture that you liked?
Work is nothing but problems.	Exactly what kind of problems are you having at work?
There are no solutions.	In what ways have you tried to solve the problem?

96

In your next online discussion, write down examples of comments that leave out words or have vague pronouns, verbs, or nouns. Then write down examples of questions that could help clarify the comments.

STATEMENTS	QUESTIONS
1. _____	_____
2. _____	_____
3. _____	_____
4. _____	_____
5. _____	_____
6. _____	_____
7. _____	_____
8. _____	_____
9. _____	_____
10. _____	_____

LEARNING COMMUNITIES IN ONLINE CLASSROOMS

HOLLY McCRACKEN

In this chapter, you will learn about:

- How the strength of online learning is the development of a rich learning community
- How to effectively engage in the online learning community

As an online student, you will quickly realize that the interaction that occurs in a virtual classroom is more important to learning than it is in a traditional classroom. Communication with learning peers as well as instructors is the essential medium for developing rich and meaningful learning experiences in web-based classes. Although online students may initially come to virtual classrooms for convenience, they return because of the connections they make to mentors, advisers, instructors, and peers. As one online student, Bill Paolini of Maryland, explains:

> The sense of community makes the learning experience feel real and tangible. . . . If there is no community then all we get out of the experience is information. For information to become knowledge it needs to be grounded in discussion, interaction, and experiences with others. . . . Information, knowledge, understanding, and wisdom only have usefulness in the context of a society.

This chapter focuses on participation in active online learning communities. Online learning communities are formed through ongoing discussion. They are essential to helping you meet your individual learning needs, and to achieving goals shared with peers.

VIRTUALLY ANYTHING CAN HAPPEN ONLINE!

Effective online instructors work collaboratively with students to carefully and intentionally shape learning communities, realizing that online courses that lack in communal aspects are much less engaging and challenging than community-rich courses. The online learning environment is learner-centered, so a lack of community really detracts from the learning possibilities. The goal is to find the virtual classroom a dynamic, interactive environment in which learning opportunities are limited only by imagination, skills, and technology. A dynamic, learner-centered online classroom can include:

- Conference telephone calls with the author of your textbook and an audio conference with peers in an asynchronous discussion forum
- "Panel discussions" by academic and professional experts from around the world, joining participants in a synchronous chat to discuss real-world issues related to the course
- Virtual learning teams that complete a group project, using a combination of asynchronous, threaded discussions and synchronous whiteboards and chat rooms
- Internships in your home town where you discuss your experience with other interns from around the country, reviewing a combination of preposted lecture notes and participating in real-time, text-based discussions
- Virtual conferences, participating in a real-time, object-oriented virtual environment for a text-based conversation with attendees from around the world
- Collaborative research with global colleagues, communicating through chat, email, telephone, and interactive video to compare findings

Online discussion is the means to ensure that opportunities for information sharing, collaboration, self-assessment, and networking are accessible in the virtual classroom. In short, communication, interaction, discussion, and dialogue are the ways by which you are visible—participating in a community that helps you meet your individual needs as well as course goals. As the community develops, you will encourage each other, identifying unique ways to meet group and individual learning needs, and using each other as resources for an ongoing exploration of course information.

As another online learner, Rebecca Walker of North Carolina, notes, "I wouldn't be able to learn all I have without the sense of community. Other learners motivate me and remind me that there are other perspectives besides my own."

There are many ways online students can communicate together, and you will learn much more as you become involved in interactive learning activities. You should expect to be involved in group discussions and team projects, not just sitting in front of a computer screen and reading, as is widely misunderstood. For instance, your instructor might ask you to do the following:

- Introduce yourself to others in the class by posting a brief biography
- Answer discussion questions and respond to the comments of peers
- Read a text-based lecture, write a response, and post it in a discussion forum
- Meet online with peers over a period of weeks to collaborate on a project, ultimately presenting it to the larger learning community
- Participate in "Webquests," enhancing Web-based research skills
- Complete research and share your experiences online with class members
- Assist peers with assessment of writing assignments by sending your feedback to them via email
- Work with classmates through the use of peer-to-peer technology applications, sharing files, Web sites, and other data sources to accomplish common goals

To be successful online and to demonstrate knowledge and skill acquisition through participation in these types of online activities, your comments will need to integrate experiences, readings, and observations, and be informed and reflective, indicating your ability to think critically.

HOW ONLINE LEARNING COMMUNITIES DEVELOP

Just as a physical classroom requires the use of tools such as blackboards or chalk to communicate and teach course content, a virtual classroom utilizes elements to help you integrate developing skills, knowledge, and abilities. Most online classrooms use some type of electronic conferencing tool that allows for *asynchronous* and *synchronous* communication. Asynchronous discussion, commonly used in virtual classrooms, allows ongoing participation, independent of a fixed time or location. Asynchronous discussions are organized by creating discussion threads, or message sequences consisting of an original message followed by multiple responses. For example, your instructor will post a message consisting of an original discussion question. You respond to that question by replying to the message. Your "posting" or response is saved or "archived" for reference in the online course. Many systems will also include a mechanism allowing synchronous discussions—conversations dependent upon participation in "real" time.

However, there is a great deal more to developing online learning communities than being able navigate a Web site. A virtual community develops on a variety of levels with regard to roles, responsibilities, cohesiveness, relational depth, capacity for cooperation, and collaboration. A community progresses through a range of stages as demonstrated by the individual behaviors, ideas, and feelings of members. The passages between stages can impact the ways online members accomplish both individual and collective goals, and ultimately, the extent to which they are successful in an online course.

ADVANTAGES AND DISADVANTAGES OF STAYING CONNECTED ONLINE

Successful participation in virtual communities depends upon many variables: software stability, hardware availability, connectivity, and even your own skill level using conferencing. Even though conferencing mechanisms have variable strengths to enhance interaction in online classrooms, their use can also pose obstacles for students and instructors alike. Table 10.1 examines the advantages and disadvantages of the online learning environment.

WAYS YOUR ONLINE INSTRUCTOR CAN HELP

Your instructor can help you overcome any disadvantages you experience online. He or she can use a variety of media and methods to communicate course content and interact with you, both individually and as a member of the larger group, using virtual whiteboards, threaded discussions, chat applications, email, or private discussions. The instructor can clearly state the purpose of the learning community and discussions as they relate to course content, and facilitate communications by asking questions or making comments that will assist you in making important connections to people, ideas, or resources. Likewise, he or she can identify inappropriate use of the discussion forum. Although electronic communications are stored online, you have the right to expect a level of privacy in order to proceed in the discussion, as well as to know who will be reviewing discussion transcripts and for what reasons, and your instructor can provide this information to you.

Expect your instructor to develop specific strategies to encourage communication and interaction, provide clear expectations for participation, offer guidance regarding course navigation, and include clear procedures in order to ensure that the discussion is consistently focused, relevant, and purposeful. For example, here are a few things your online instructor can do:

TABLE 10.1   **Benefits and Disadvantages of the Online Environment**

BENEFITS OF ONLINE ENVIRONMENT	DISADVANTAGES OF ONLINE ENVIRONMENT
1. Learners have continuous, equal, and individual access to instructors, online peers, and learning resources.	1. Learners must know how to use technical tools and how to obtain technical assistance.
2. The environment provides a self-paced atmosphere for reflection, composition, and analysis, enabling you to prepare considered and researched responses.	2. The environment is often limited to asynchronous activities since it cannot take advantage of coordinated schedules.
3. It encourages active involvement through interaction and collaboration, assisting you to integrate new ideas, skills, and areas of knowledge.	3. Its use may be especially challenging in the absence of facial expressions, voice intonation, or eye contact.
4. It facilitates communication between you and others from a wide range of backgrounds; its anonymity enables open expression without stereotyping based on appearance, physical ability, gender, race, or class.	4. Communication occurs at unequal levels because participants may vary widely in their abilities to express themselves in writing, and to maintain focus on relevant discussion issues.
5. Environment allows communications that you can revise and retrieve for ongoing reference.	5. Environment can reinforce insecurity and vulnerability among online students, noting that transcripts can be archived and confidentiality cannot be ensured.
6. Environment reinforces the continued use of evolving technology applications, allowing students to build skills and abilities for studying and conducting Web-based research.	6. Because communication is conveyed through the written word, it may present obstacles to students with reading, writing, keyboarding, or vision challenges.
7. It allows you to work independently, but enables you to consult with instructors and peers as you choose.	7. It relies heavily on peer exchange, frustrating those who learn only from subject matter experts.
8. Participation is not restricted to a time/location specific class schedule; you have any time/any place access to learning environments.	8. Its use demands that online students acquire text-based facilitation, communication, and information management competencies in order to manage messages.

Adapted from: Vicki Phillips (Ed.). (2002). The importance of virtual learning communities to motivating and retaining online learners. In Holly McCracken, *Motivating and retaining online learners. GetEducated.Com.*

- Be available, aware that teaching in a Web-based classroom requires that the instructor be easily accessible and responsive.
- Understand that you might be self-conscious regarding the quality and quantity of your contributions to the discussion, particularly during the first few weeks of class.
- Be able to use the technology characteristic to virtual communication and discussions, and be prepared to help you troubleshoot if you experience problems.
- Create a schedule for exchanging communications and state when you should post assignments for each unit of study.
- Facilitate discussions, explaining their purpose and goals, and provide guidelines for proceeding.
- Let you know the minimum expectations for participation and how it will affect your grade or progress.
- Provide guidelines for interaction, privacy, and conflict management.
- Monitor how you're doing, and provide ongoing feedback to ensure that you have a consistently positive learning experience.
- Use the wealth of information available via the Internet to recommend new resources for further discussion, information, or study.
- Consider the range of learning styles present in the discussion. While the online learning environment is largely a text-based one, he or she can provide types of activities that respond to a range of learning styles.

You will know that the online learning community is developing positively if class communication increases with comments around self-assessment, personal disclosure, or the evaluation of one another's work. These types of discussions will expand on course themes, and will generate problem solving, resource sharing, and academic or professional networking.

Likewise, your instructor should be watching to see if anyone is at risk of being unsuccessful in meeting learning goals through their lack of participation. For example, students should be made aware of neglecting assignments or being absent from discussions. Your online instructor can also note the quantity of your communications as well as the quality of your remarks and interaction. For example, your responses should indicate interest, research, and application, and demonstrate to your instructor that you understand and can use course information. References to the text and page numbers are useful ways of communicating your understanding of material to the instructor. Your instructor will pay attention to noticeable changes in how often you are present in the class and how much you contribute to discussions. He or she will specifically note repeated references to problems that interfere with ongoing participation, such as continued challenges to access or writing, editing, keyboarding, reading, or vision difficulties. The continuing presence of these issues may indicate that you are struggling with course information and materials.

WAYS TO CONTRIBUTE TO THE ONLINE LEARNING COMMUNITY

Unlike being in a physical classroom, it's difficult to sit quietly in the back row in an online class. In order to have the most valuable experience possible, use discussions to demonstrate that you are an active, self-directed, disciplined, and motivated student and community member. There are some specific actions you can take in order to make a strong and enthusiastic start in your class, and to make the most out of participating in an online learning community. Consider the following:

Make Sure That Your Instructor Can Contact You

Provide your instructor with your most recent email addresses and your phone number, and inform the instructor immediately of changes.

Stay Up-to-Date in Discussions

One of the advantages of online learning is that one is actually able to "learn any time, any place." However, although the medium used—the online environment—is asynchronous, many courses follow a traditional academic calendar. Your instructor will provide you with a schedule that tells you when and how often you should participate in discussions.

Return to the Discussion

Throughout each week, participate in a discussion at least five times weekly to see what others have written. Be "present" in the class on a regular basis. Take part in the discussions and be a part of the community. Frequent communications not only build cooperative relationships, they are critical to developing learning communities with unique depth and focus.

Help Organize the Online Classroom

By carefully labeling postings in the subject line of your responses, your messages can be easily accessed and referenced in the threaded discussion outline.

Don't Let Technology Problems Wait

If you are having problems with the technological aspects of taking an online course, contact the school's technical support unit to help you solve software and hardware problems.

Let Your Class Know What Your Thoughts Are

Share your particular insights to questions by illustrating examples with individual experiences. Your responses will be unique and personal, and demonstrate that you understand course information.

Ask for Help If You Need It

If you are unclear about an assignment or particular activity, or experience difficulties as you proceed with the course, ask for assistance. Knowing when to ask for help and how to formulate questions to get the information you need are important skills to develop as an online student.

Stay in Touch with Your Instructor

If you are unclear about a question, issue, or expectation, don't wait. Information, activities, discussions, and assignments are sequenced; therefore, it is important that you clarify any questions or concerns as quickly as possible.

Consider the Personality You Create

Through written communication and interaction, ensure that your communication accurately reflects your personality—intentions, values, and insights. An understanding of each other's lives and experiences, and a joint interest in the subject, constitute a strong cyber community.

Take Time to Respond

Be genuine and informed; this includes being mindful of spelling, punctuation, and grammar as you participate in text-based discussions. Your instructor and learning peers will appreciate thoughtful and detailed participation. This indicates that you take communication and discussion seriously, that you understand the function of the community in an online course, and that you view your study as a collaborative process.

Respect Your Learning Community

Even though you can "attend class in your pajamas," you are obligated to maintain the same standards for polite communication in an online classroom that you would in its face-to-face counterpart. Show consideration for the individual privacy of community members, acknowledging individual boundaries, specific requests, and needs, and respecting mutually agreed upon procedures regarding disclosure of discussion content.

Enjoy the Members of the Community

Without a community, you would be working in an isolation booth. An active online learning community is not the same thing as a correspondence course. It takes strong motivation to encourage a student to continue in such an isolated environment. Try to enjoy reading all of the responses made by other students, and learn from them. Don't be afraid just to chat with the other online students—it doesn't all have to be class related. Even if you took a "live" class, you probably wouldn't get as much opportunity to know the other students and share their thoughts on the subject as we do in online classes.

Capitalize on the Benefits of the Online Classroom

For example, one of the noted benefits to online learning is its capacity for anonymity. Students self-conscious about speaking openly in a face-to-face class may capitalize on this aspect as a means to more fearless and assertive participation.

Be Patient

Give your learning peers time to develop a proficiency in the skills required for successful navigation in the virtual classroom.

Take Risks

Almost all students are hesitant to participate in class discussions, feeling self-conscious about their interpretations of topics or questions, the ways they have phrased feedback to others, or their writing abilities in general. Don't let fear or lack of confidence interfere with taking the initiative to participate.

Forgive Mistakes

We all make them. If you do not understand someone's intent, phraseology, purpose, or language, ask for clarification. This may prevent miscommunications or "flames" from breaking out of control in a text-based, asynchronous environment.

CONCLUSION

When given the choice between simply reading one-dimensional text on a computer screen or interacting in dynamic online learning community discussions with peers from across the globe, the votes are in. Communication and interaction provide important aspects of online learning and development.

What's in it for you? As an online student, you get the experience of talking with students from around the world, reaching resources from experts in your field in a matter of minutes, and staying in continuous contact with your instructor and peers, all in your own time and at your own pace.

As one online learner, Masha Malka, confirmed, *"A good learning community has great power. It makes learning a lot more effective—it makes learning happen!"*

APPLICATION EXERCISE 10A

Working in an Online Learning Community or Alone

There are reasons for working in an online learning community as well as for working alone. List your reasons for working in each situation.

REASONS FOR WORKING IN AN ONLINE LEARNING COMMUNITY

- You get additional ideas from your peers.

  ____

  ____

  ____

- They help you identify your mistakes.

  ____

  ____

  ____

- Explaining things to peers helps you learn.

  ____

  ____

  ____

  ____

  ____

  ____

  ____

  ____

REASONS FOR WORKING ALONE

- You don't want your responses to assignments influenced by others.

  _____

  _____

  _____

- If you share a task, you have to depend on other people.

  _____

  _____

  _____

- You work differently than other people.

  _____

  _____

  _____

  _____

  _____

  _____

  _____

  _____

  _____

CHAPTER 11

WORKING IN ONLINE GROUPS

DEANA L. MOLINARI

In this chapter, you will learn about:

- The benefits of online groups
- Types of online groups
- Phases of the online group process
- How to help develop successful online groups

> *"The strength of the wolf is in the pack."*
> Rudyard Kipling

> *"I find it difficult to finish my day's work, care for my family, and then face the blinking cursor all by myself."*
> Anonymous Online Student

Students in a traditional college classroom experience the same kinds of learning challenges as their online peers. In both settings, students must organize the educational task, solve the problems, and relate to one another. On the other hand, the online setting also requires that students relate to one another through a computer. Although some students like to learn alone, others learn better with others. This need for other people is especially felt when one feels deprived of typical social contacts, particularly trying to relate to students through technology. In addition, most distance-learning students have busy lives—family, work, and school. These responsibilities press hard on available time and emotional resources.

If an online student knows no one else in a similar situation, isolation can feel so heavy that continuation of the course seems impossible. Even reading a syllabus without someone else can be a difficult task. Sometimes, trying to match the assignments to the texts is a challenge. It is even more challenging if the school has sent you the wrong books for the course. It seems quite natural that new online students might assume that they are ones who are ignorant, and quit the online course before it even begins.

The online group discussion helps solve many of the problems of isolation, and increases learning as well. In this chapter you will learn the benefits of online groups, types of groups, the phases of group process, and how to help develop successful online groups.

ONLINE GROUP BENEFITS

The need to work and learn in groups seems ingrained in humans. Work done by several people is often better than individually conceived solutions. The group redefines the educational experience by more fully integrating the instructor, the process, the student, and the outcome. For example, in an online writing class, six groups can be given the challenge to describe an object without naming it. Each group acts as the instructor when their units define different objects (a watch, a hearing aid, a gyroscope). They detail the challenge and assign individuals tasks and deadlines. The completed descriptions are then given to different groups to solve and critique. The groups have to set standards and methods to complete the critiquing assignment.

The online group enhances the learning process because it requires students to interact with one another—learning about content, the Internet, how to relate to others, and how to write in groups. The group requires students to ask questions, challenge assumptions, research topics, make decisions, and summarize progress. Group identity enhances student participation and the individual thinking process. Online students enter with one set of ideas and leave with another. In the meantime, friendships develop, emotions are shared, and understanding expands. Groups even become competitive about their outcome products much like school or sports team membership.

In one online group, students produced statement papers on health policy. Then they had to analyze the arguments of other papers and vote on the best arguments. The online discussions revealed that people could often not see past their own papers. Individual biases prevented objective analysis of logical arguments. The online group members learned more as they collectively discussed and reviewed basic principles about structuring arguments and evaluating arguments. Online group work prevented personal opinions from blocking the learning experience.

Online groups bring diverse students together. Some degree programs are completely online and combine students from all over the country into one class. In these cases, the online group is more convenient than the weekend seminar. Students do not have to travel, find babysitters, or arrange replacements for work. The online group is also less expensive than traveling, and it means not having to leave the security of one's house. The online group brings diversity to the class not frequently found in most brick-and-mortar classrooms.

One major benefit of online group learning is the melding of diverse thought. For instance, a rural health online class brought together people from Alabama, California, Florida, Montana, Utah, Washington, DC, and England. As these students discussed health topics, they discovered both geographical similarities and differences in their concerns. They each held a different definition of "rural" but ultimately agreed on solutions. They shared ideas and methods. The give-and-take of ideas animated the learning process. Such online discussion can prove more valuable than a textbook.

Online groups also allow students to become more "vocal." In face-to-face classrooms, the instructor often directs the topics of discussion, the direction of the discussion, and its length. Online group discussion customizes the learning. No two groups are alike. The group decides what is important to discuss and how much to say. In online education, the more effort and communication you put into the group process, the more motivation, excitement, connection, and learning occurs.

TYPES OF ONLINE GROUPS

Communication tools greatly influence how the online group works. If the group works in a *threaded discussion* format, a more formal process develops. Participation requires going to the threaded discussion place much as students are required to go to a classroom. Online students are required to reply to a particular message and the discussion moves on from there. Some online students like this since it gives a routine to class participation. For instance, when students take a face-to-face class, they dress in a certain way, travel to a certain location, take their books, enter a room, and may even sit in the same seat each time. These routines ease the difficulty of learning. Threaded discussion can do the same thing with online classes. Threaded discussion is one way to ritualize an online class. The subject line formats the message. The format keeps similar messages together so that the discussion "unfolds" like an outline. Threaded discussion keeps different topics together in different geographical spaces, requiring jumping from place to place to find the latest contributions. Often, online classes that use this format have a separate place for "chat" discussions. Online students can experience a task-oriented formal discussion or an informal conversation with other students.

Automated Email

This organizes classes in a different fashion. The postal analogy gives the group a more personal nature. Online students go into their email to see their messages. Students read messages on a "first come, first read" basis. The problem with this method is the lack of organization if people do not use the subject line to "thread" or organize the discussion. Online students must learn to "filter" their mail in order to keep the incoming class messages together, and prevent overwhelming the regular inbox.

Online instructors use communication tools for a variety of purposes such as talking with experts, regulating tasks, meeting place for teams, cooperatives, and interdependent groups.

Online Communities

Online communities are groups of people interested in the same topic. Individuals contribute their expertise to questions asked by others. Professional groups often support these communities. Online students can benefit from a community's expertise. For example, medical students can join a professional interest community group so that they can learn what the latest trends are, and even ask the experts about topics that are too new to appear in journals and texts.

A Learning Team Approach

This permits small numbers of people to work together inside a larger class structure. The online team may work on assignments together such as researching the Internet, but individuals can also work alone and receive an individual grade. Sometimes online courses use the team approach in an attempt to bring more social interaction to the class. For example, an online capstone class can separate students into teams by professions—business, health, technology, and so on. General assignments can be given to the teams, but each team brings the issues and concerns of their profession to the task. In addition, such teams can serve as networking opportunities for students in the same field, a major advantage after graduation.

An Online Cooperative Group

This group requires students to solve a problem together. The cooperative group usually defines the problem, divides it, and then individuals work alone on parts of the project, and contribute their work to a final project. But such groups require a great deal of individual responsibility. For example, an undergraduate online nursing class was required to write research papers. The groups spent time interpreting the assignment requirements, breaking down the group roles, and dividing the work between group members. They divided the work by topics and paper sections. Before the deadline, students submitted their work to a group editor, who put the paper together. Such group work is not without difficulties. In one group, a few members did not submit their sections by the deadline, which didn't allow time for a group review and editing before the paper was sent to the instructor. One member felt frustrated by the final product, observing, "My contribution was misquoted and incorrectly edited. There were major overall English grammar and spelling problems."

The Interdependent Online Group

The Interdependent Online Group is a more involved and cooperative group. This type of group works on a more abstract problem that takes more time, resources, and minds to solve. There may not be one right answer. The interdependent group depends upon the expertise of each group member to address the problem. Each member of the group is vital to the project. No student shirks duties without being noticed. Students communicate often and seek one another's advice in problem solving. Interdisciplinary online classes often use this type of class. Online graduate courses in business and health utilize this type of problem solving because it mimics real life. A great deal of communication is required to keep people up to date with progress and problems. The cycle of defining, assessing, exploring, summarizing, and deciding moves the online group ever closer to their final product.

In one example of an interdependent online group, accounting, marketing, management and behavior organization majors came together to build a business solution. Students first identified what they needed to know before they could proceed. They then searched for resources to help learn what they did not know. They found that relationships must be dependable, and preferably pleasant, in order for a group like this to succeed. Relationship-building and maintenance skills are mandatory.

COLLABORATIVE GROUP PHASES

Online group members are more likely to succeed when they elucidate their interests, identify necessary resources, recognize possible goal obstacles, specify procedures to follow, and satisfy the task requirements. Effective online students understand that the collaborative process can enhance the learning process by making sure that all the steps are included. Dr. Laurie Nelson from the University of Indiana developed a collaboration theory after observing expert collaborators. She divides their process into three phases: preparation, work, and closure.

The Preparation Phase

Preparation accomplishes several tasks, including getting ready, organizing the groups, agreeing on the problem, and establishing group roles. The getting ready portion of the process establishes a common base from which the group moves forward. Online members review the collaborative process by practicing group process skills and communication processes. In this phase, online members do an overview of the project in order to understand what is expected. Before the students finally agree on the problem, they will brainstorm and review as many alternative solutions as possible.

Identifying needed roles and assigning them completes the preparation phase of online collaboration. The online group process requires students to perform different roles. Sometimes the online instructor defines the roles, but most of the time the roles are implicit. Roles can be defined by their functions:

- Decision making
- Creativity
- Relationship issues
- Process issues

The variety of the roles enables everyone to be a leader, and students can take on more than one role. Roles can and should shift throughout the longer process. Online group work is more functional when roles are shared.

For the new online student, there are a few important pitfalls to avoid. First, you must address any fear of unseen people and fear of offending others. Respect is a crucial part of the online environment, but group members must be prepared to "speak up" and disagree politely if necessary. Second, you must work to understand the group roles needed to accomplish the task. This involves getting a clear sense of the task and the talents available in the group. Taking more than a week to assign roles prevents the group from working as effectively and efficiently as it can. When people don't know what to do, they do nothing. Remember, time is a greater challenge to the online group process than it is to a face-to-face group.

The Work Phase

Work comes next. Members perform their assigned roles, plan, complete the work, and finalize the project. Each person must contribute often or the group fails. Online groups where everyone contributes ideas, asks questions, reminds the group of deadlines, and summarizes process produce more comprehensive outcomes than those in which just a few students send a message. There are more alternatives to choose from when people contribute more.

Closure

This is the last phase of the online group process. Issues such as evaluating the group's process, alternative solutions, and the final product have been technically satisfied. Now the levels of involvement determine the amount and type of closure needed. Some online projects require only a "so long" to close. Other online groups require deeper member involvement. Students may be reluctant to end their relationships with the closure of the project. A celebration of the group's process may be needed. Online parties may not include pizza and soda, but jokes, praise, and socialization can occur.

DEVELOPING SUCCESSFUL ONLINE GROUPS

Successful online groups require more than just task-centered skills such as information sharing, information seeking, and meaning making. Relationship-building skills enable online students to accomplish tasks. This section will discuss the need to develop relational skills and communication techniques.

"Distance" in distant education can mean both geographical and emotional remoteness unless major efforts are taken to prevent problems. The nature of online communication requires people using a computer to relate with words. Writers paint emotion with symbols, while readers interpret the many emotional colors using black-and-white words. In face-to-face groups, people use visual social methods to link with others. Although the words fly and disappear, body language continues the emotional links. In the computer-mediated world, the words stay while the person disappears. Hence, handling one's emotions in an online course requires new skills. Online students may feel less constrained, as well as anonymous, unseen, and dehumanized. Feelings for others can be altered. The person at the other end of the computer can seem two-dimensional, like a television character, so that empathy can be harder to develop. Online students can find it easier to feel upset by what others write because they read between the lines, often misinterpreting another student's intent.

In face-to-face situations, sarcasm can be an acceptable form of humor. Body language, facial gestures, and tone of voice can be "read" to discover the friendly humor behind the remarks. But in the online culture, apparent sarcasm reads as an attack. One online student was so upset by a suggestion that her facilitator made that she wanted to quit. The facilitator said, "The group needs to explore new ideas and spend less time making decisions." The student mulled over the comment and grew angrier. She thought about how the instructor did not praise them for what they were doing right. She nurtured the anger until it incapacitated her. The student refused to speak with the instructor and went to a supervisor to complain. Once she was able to speak with the instructor, the comments were clarified and the anger defused. The student was able to return to the group process. But made in a face-to-face environment, the instructor's comment might have been interpreted as advice, rather than as a negative complaint. Traditional students can observe body language, ask questions, and move forward to the next topic—a more complicated matter for the online student.

The constraints of the online medium foster the development of new methods of communication. Some online instructors require posting your personal biography in order to open up interpersonal communication. Online students may interview one another and then post the interviews. Other icebreakers also enable online students to overcome the fears common to all new classes and groups. Posting pictures, sharing Web page addresses, making a personal Web page, or telling about one's most embarrassing moment can break the ice. Some online instructors ask questions such as "Why did you register for this class?" or "Tell about your worst or best experience with (the class content)."

In the online classroom, the sharing of self may be just as important as the task. Online groups increase retention by bringing a sense of collegiality to the learning experience. Without this, online classes can have a high dropout rate. Online students are left to find their own motivations for completing "hard" or "boring" course assignments. Online group identity can promote student motivation, interest, and accountability.

The importance of the first online communication cannot be overemphasized. The first communication initiates the online culture of the group or class. The "follow the leader" syndrome is a term for patterning one's messaging by looking at others' messages. Since the online group's rules are set in the first communication, tone, length, type of discussion, depth of thinking, and use of resources can be defined in this message. If the first message is too social in content, others may follow the example and ultimately produce a poor group product. If the first message is too task-oriented, the online group may never form an identity or become a cohesive unit. Balance is necessary. It is most effective to include both social and task elements in your online messages.

Validation

This is a crucial online skill that helps create effective groups. There are many ways to validate other online students. Using social greetings to begin messages sets a communal tone. Addressing people by their names, agreeing with others with specific comments about their major points, or even disagreeing with ideas but using facts to do so are all ways of showing respect for each other. Without the typical nonverbals of face-to-face communication, online students appreciate encouragement and praise. Online validation of others encourages more messages and a feeling of safety in expression. For example, if you are worried about one person's progress, you can send a personal email, asking something like "Are you OK? I miss hearing from you. Anything I can do to help?" This approach helps online students who are having problems and just need a personal touch to help them re-enter the process. Consider the following tips:

- The more you put into the online group, the more connection you will feel.
- Use the subject line to keep the online discussion organized.
- Express your ideas about the group's progress in a positive manner.
- Go overboard to explain what you mean.
- Use positive emotional expression to phrase even your worst frustrations.
- Use words—emoticons are not always understood by others and fail to express feelings properly.
- Ask for clarification on anything that stirs negative emotions; do not sit upon the emotion until it "hatches."
- Greet other online students in an informal and personal way.
- Share something about your personal study process.
- Ask for help. Do not suffer alone—someone out there has an answer.

CONCLUSION

Working in an online group can be an exciting challenge. The online group enables students who might otherwise not be able to meet together and discuss new ideas. Communication structures the type of online discussion that takes place. Knowledge of online communication can help you to succeed. An understanding of the online collaborative process can help you to problem solve and manage online relationships effectively. Having a variety of online strategies will help you to feel safer and to accomplish your educational goals. Good luck!

APPLICATION EXERCISE 11A

Contributing to the Online Group Process

In order to help you become an effective online group member, use this checklist to evaluate your knowledge and skills:

- Have you determined the purpose of the online group?

  ____

  ____

  ____

- What are your opinions on the online process and task?

  ____

  ____

  ____

- Are you listening with an open mind to what other students have to say?

  ____

  ____

  ____

- Are you contributing and making your opinions known to the online group?

  ____

  ____

  ____

- Are you keeping your cool during any conflict and responding to other students with respect and understanding? Would you be OK if you received your own messages?

  _____

  _____

  _____

- Can you state the online group's purpose to the other students?

  _____

  _____

  _____

- Are you eliciting contributions from other online group members?

  _____

  _____

  _____

- Are you helping the online group to reach consensus or are you an obstacle?

  _____

  _____

  _____

- Are you helping to keep the morale of the online group positive?

  _____

  _____

  _____

DEALING WITH ONLINE CONFLICT

KEN W. WHITE

In this chapter, you will learn about:

- Online conflict as communication
- Benefits of online conflict
- Types of online conflict
- Responding effectively to online conflict

Some level of frustration and controversy is normal fare for online students. You will often encounter difficult students who may dominate a class discussion, display rude and inappropriate tone to other class members, or refuse to adhere to the class structure. In addition, if conflicts are bad enough and are ignored long enough, the results can end up a disastrous "flame war" in a class. The real task at hand is responding effectively to online conflicts before they get to the point where your learning and success are affected.

Although disagreement and conflict are inevitable aspects of all human relationships, the need to respond effectively in online conflict situations is particularly important. Students interacting on computers are isolated from social cues and feel safe from surveillance and criticism. As a consequence of the low level of nonverbal and social information available online, messages are often startlingly blunt and discussions can easily escalate into name-calling and other forms of abusive and contemptuous behavior. Such *flaming* messages do not go unremarked, and can be met with numerous reactions that resort to even stronger language. Before the online student is even aware of a flame war, the social fabric and learning climate of the class can be severely damaged.

In an online environment where students feel less bound by convention and less concerned with consequences, conflict can erupt frequently. Sources of conflict have to be identified and responded to as effectively as possible. Understanding and learning must be maintained in the online classroom.

The focus of this chapter is on helping online students respond effectively to online conflict. To begin, I make a distinction between "reacting" and "responding." I associate reactive behavior with the concept of "movement." It's like a physical process we find in nature. Like movement, reacting is reflexive—it's fight or flight. On the other hand, I consider responsive behavior more like the concept of "action." It's a human practice involving thinking and choice. That is, responding is reflective. Unlike reptiles who react, humans are "response-able," able to respond.

Online conflict is addressed effectively through communication. If we "react" to conflict, we ignore or cancel out one or more of the crucial communication elements of conflict. By recognizing those communication elements, we can eliminate "reactive" or ineffective ways of communicating through online conflict and begin to "respond" effectively. We can benefit from reflecting on our own attitudes about conflict and on our own communication skills, because while all online conflict is not rooted in poor communication, it always involves communication.

The starting point for responding effectively to online conflict is to ask yourself what it is you want to have happen. Focus on what is positive, specific, and practical. To begin, online conflicts can be responded to effectively by looking at three key areas: (1) what online conflict is and how it works, including its benefits, (2) the different types of online conflict, and (3) what online students can do about each type.

ONLINE CONFLICT AS COMMUNICATION

There are two initial lessons for online learning. First, there are many grounds for conflict. Whenever people are involved in interdependent and interactive relationships, such as in the online classroom, there are many situations over which conflicts can arise. Second, it may be quite challenging to get a handle on the complex and often subjective dynamics of conflict, particularly in the online classroom.

Consequently, the initial step in responding effectively to conflict situations is to know what the conflict is about and how it works. Once you've made some sense out of conflict and its communication dynamics, you are better able to figure out what you can do about it. I want to offer a communication-oriented definition of conflict that suggests specific ways for communicating through online conflicts.

I agree with John Stewart of the University of Washington when he defines "conflict" in his book *Together: Communicating Interpersonally* as communication—verbally and nonverbally expressed disagreement between individuals or groups. Though broad, Stewart's definition allows us to say several particular things about conflict. First, the definition points out that conflict is expressed with words or through nonverbal behaviors such as writing in all caps, an important factor in online communication. Sometimes online students use words to express their disagreement by writing, "I disagree with what you are saying!" At other times, it's the lack of words and participation that clearly signal disagreement.

Second, when seen as communication, conflict is "expressed," as opposed to "being feelings" that happen inside a person. The definition concentrates on communication. It doesn't encourage us to speculate about or interpret the motives of the person on the other end of the computer, but to focus on how we both communicate. It reminds us that conflict is always about a relationship between two or more people.

Third, and most importantly, the definition emphasizes that conflict is a natural part of human interaction. Conflict is essentially about different points of views. People have disagreements because they are different. Because we are not the same, and because we see and value things differently, we vary in our beliefs as to what things are or should be. While conflict may divert time and energy away from tasks, represent the various issues that polarize individuals and groups within organizations, and obstruct cooperative action and decrease productivity, it is also a creative and positive force.

It is important to recognize that, as communication, online conflict has some benefits.

BENEFITS OF ONLINE CONFLICT

If online conflict is inevitable and natural—if it represents the uniqueness of all people—then it is not always negative. A major part of the problem about responding effectively to online conflict is our tendency to think only about the negative part of it. We need to begin seeing the benefits of online conflict.

The list of positive and creative values inherent in online conflict is equally long. Conflict has the potential to:

- Open up hidden issues
- Clarify subject-matter
- Improve the quality of problem solving
- Increase involvement in learning
- Increase cooperation and interaction

Online conflicts can be valuable and productive both for online faculty and students. For the online instructor, conflict can stimulate creative problem solving, generate more effective ideas, and fine-tune learning relationships.

For online students, conflict can provide opportunities to test, expand, and demonstrate skills, better understand their co-learners, and develop confidence and trust.

The Opportunity for Interpersonal Online Relationships

A legitimate disagreement can bring a potential for human understanding to the online classroom. Conflict can help us learn something new about one another and remind us of one another's humanity. We can develop understanding that goes beyond the subject matter of what we're learning to an appreciation of who we are. For example, let's say that there is a hidden conflict in an online ethics class about some students imposing their religious beliefs on others. In a discussion about the range of ethical theories, Richard declares that Christianity is the only true ethical viewpoint. He shares his Christian beliefs in every note he sends to the class discussion. He shows no sensitivity to other perspectives. Another student, John, is "silent" in the class, but eventually sends the instructor a personal message and writes in no uncertain terms, "If you don't stop this guy, I'm going to give him hell!"

The online instructor could avoid the possible benefit of conflict in this situation by making an "executive decision" and ordering the class as a whole to respect all opinions and not to share their personal moral views. Instead, the instructor sends Richard a personal message and poses the problem to him. He describes the feeling and frustrations of the other students, notes one student's reluctance to join in the discussion, and asks how the situation should be handled. In response, Richard writes back that he does have strong beliefs, that he was not aware of the feelings of the other students, and that he will try to be less pushy. The instructor then supplements his communication with a telephone call to Richard, thanking him for his productive response and talking in more general terms about how the class is going, what's the weather's like in Richard's hometown, and sharing personal information about jobs and family.

This example shows how online students often lack tangible reminders of their audience. Lacking the face-to-face resources to help convey ideas, online students often resort to even stronger language to express passion of belief.

Without a face to remind him of his audience and to temper his words, Richard forgot about convention and consequences. He needed to be reminded of the interpersonal element without increasing the sense of isolation that is common online. The instructor accomplished this by focusing on Richard's humanity as well. Consequently, one result of the conflict was about tasks: a working relationship was formed. But a second result was even more important: Richard realized that he didn't handle the interpersonal part of the online conflict very well—he didn't remind himself of the person on the other end of the computer.

‍lict over Values

‍ive online instructors recognize that online classes are part of social
‍izations as well as places where people accomplish individual and col-
‍ tasks. Over time, most organizations develop a culture that strongly
‍the way people view their place of work, its management, and its pri-
‍urposes. Although culture in organizations is defined as the common
‍ of both managers and employees, cultural values are not imposed.
‍re developed over time. There can be disagreements over organiza-
‍values, such as over the level of expectations of all members of the
‍d regarding what service to customers means. In fact, conflict over
‍ values may be necessary. Communication and human relations in
‍ations with well-defined, positive cultural values are nearly always
‍han in those that pay little attention to the values of the organization.
‍value in communicating through conflict about organizational val-
‍they are most effectively dealt with in a structured way where there
‍ortunity for mutual respect, for learning, and for maintaining inter-
‍relationships.

‍suggested above, the values of various online programs differ. For
‍is "education" a value? It is clear that some working adults who
‍ine programs don't really want the education—they want what the
‍ provides for them in better jobs, moving up the career ladder, and
‍ to communicate ideas. But are those the values of the particular
‍ograms they enter? If, as an online student, you enter your class
‍ above values but the instructor expects an "intellectual life," then
‍ht be a conflict over values.

‍nately, the main point is to know your conflict. Whatever the type
‍ the next step in responding effectively is knowing what to do, or
‍y knowing what not to do—reacting.

‍G TO ONLINE CONFLICT

‍ to the beginning of this chapter and the distinction made
‍eacting" and "responding," the following ways of dealing with
‍ict can be identified as "reactive." A reactive approach does not
‍enever there is disagreement, there are always four elements to
‍ (1) you, (2) the other person, (3) the topic, and (4) the climate.
‍t three elements of conflict are easy to understand. The "you" of
‍ll of us as we deal with the second part of conflict—"other" peo-
‍c, of course, is the subject of what we are talking about. On the
‍ the last element needs further explanation. The climate of a
‍e the physical environment and objects (on the phone; face to
‍itchen, office, or bedroom; the temperature of the room; over

*Conflict can show online students that they are "talking" with other people
online who have feelings, thoughts, and lives of their own.*

The Opportunity to Promote Online Decision Making

The "adversary system" of our courts operates on the assumption that truth
and justice emerge from the clash of ideas. The above example also shows
how the clash of ideas and disagreements can lead to more workable decisions in the online classroom. The online instructor was able to get Richard
to "own" the decision to temper his communication because the conflict was
posed as a problem in need of a solution, not a conflict in need of resolution.
If the instructor's decision to stop all sharing of personal moral viewpoints
had been imposed, Richard and other students would have felt "disenfranchised." They would have most certainly carried around increased feelings of
isolation and resentments about the decision that could have interfered with
future performance, cooperation, and decisions in the online classroom. The
ultimate decision got the task completed and it strengthened relationships. In
addition, Richard felt a part of the decision and was more likely to respect it.
He realized that he was part of a real—though online—community.

The Opportunity to Help Students See That Feelings Exist Online

Here I must emphasize that I am not talking about allowing online students
to flame each other. It's crucial that feelings are communicated productively
online. I am talking about opportunities to express and explain feelings
through respectful language. Online conflicts, if responded to effectively, can
be positive opportunities for getting feelings out in a medium that is mostly
assumed to be impersonal.

*Dealing with feelings shows students the human element that is always present
in the online environment.*

As the example above shows, if the energy of a feeling like anger can
be channeled into a positive communication framework, the feelings can be
used to find creative solutions and more complete human relationships.

The Opportunity to Promote Confidence in Online Learning

There is always uncertainty in a person when things really get difficult. The
first serious argument with another student is a major event. This is especially true in online learning situations where the phenomenon of flaming
suggests that communication becomes more extreme and impulsive. But the
confidence that follows a well-managed online conflict can be extremely

valuable to learning. It is often those educational encounters that avoid conflict that are ultimately the most insecure and unproductive because they remain untested. Both online students in the above example felt a new sureness, a new security, in their working relationship. Their online relationship was tested by conflict, and they had the opportunity to develop trust and confidence by learning how to communicate successfully through those conflicts. They ultimately recognized the value of the experience and the important learning that took place.

Of course, a positive attitude is the first step to responding effectively to online conflict. Online students need to begin seeing conflict as creative and productive. The second step is to recognize that online conflict comes in several types.

TYPES OF ONLINE CONFLICT

Conflict is a pervasive part of all human relationships, including those in the online classroom. In order to respond effectively to online conflict, online students also need to recognize that not all disagreement is the same. There are three basic types of online conflict: over facts or interpretations, over online roles and identities, and over values.

Conflict over Facts or Interpretations

This kind of disagreement reflects differing views over the content and expectations of an online course. They are disagreements over fact. We can disagree over the fact that Columbus landed in the New World in 1492 (which we can easily confirm or disconfirm) or we can disagree over meaning—whether he "discovered" America at all (which is a matter of interpretation). The most important question to ask yourself when dealing with this type of online conflict is: What level of conflict are you disagreeing about—fact or meaning? It makes a difference. Your syllabus may say that you are required to interact in the online class, but what does "interaction" mean? If you are always responding to other student comments with short statements such as "I agree," are you actually interacting? And what is "correct" grammar online? Should online discussions be evaluated by the same grammatical standards as more formal online assignments like term papers or case studies? Or are online discussions, although textual, more like conversations? In addition, what does "page" mean online? Is a page one screen or is it a traditional page in length? These kinds of small conflicts over facts and interpretations can be very disruptive in an online class until they are discussed and clarified.

One fundamental online conflict over facts or i[n] about what an "online class" is. Generally speaking, an accessed anywhere and anytime and makes use of co[m] deliver student learning at flexible times and places. B[u] do not require any attendance or participation and dence courses" more than structured educational ex[periences] interaction with faculty and other students, due date[s] and the kinds of materials that contribute to the course. Many online students enter programs with what an online course is and there is an immediate n of the course and the roles of faculty members and :

Conflict over Online Roles and Identities

This kind of disagreement particularly reflects diffe[rent] roles of online instructors. Cues in traditional edu[cation] social differences. An instructor lecturing at the fr[ont] ing a student in an office is a reminder of status nologies weaken social differences apparent in fa[ce] Online instructors are not awarded authority or e because instructors look the part. All online mess a certain degree because they look alike. The o apart is their content, or what William James r Without the "halo effect" of status, the compete instructor are in question from the beginning through the quality of messages and how info[r] tional students in a regular classroom might viewpoints as authority, online students tend challenge instructor opinions.

Consequently, many online conflicts ab[out] whether an instructor is considered informe[d] on who has what kind of authority with a g dents as informed is an important step in de instructor, but that is balanced against simil[ar] Many online students are working adults learned enormously from certain important well as having formal education. They hav[e] in ways other than taking courses. They ar[e] experience needs to be recognized and util why many online instructors prefer to i rather than instructors, understanding tha tionships can be understood as struggles (

the computer) but also the emotional level of the topic. For example, the emotional context of an online climate includes the lack of many nonverbals we have during face-to-face interaction.

Virginia Satir in *Peoplemaking* defines the reactive styles in these four ways: placating, pouncing, distracting, and computing.

Placating

Placating is when we ignore ourselves in online conflict. It is an example of denying that a conflict exists. It is unresponsive because it fails to acknowledge disagreement. It avoids the conflict by using statements that terminate "talk" about the conflict before the discussion has thoroughly developed. It writes in generalities and avoids specifics. When online students placate a conflict, they don't directly accept their responsibility. Often online placators "lurk" in the background of the class, simply observing and keeping their opinions to themselves.

Don't placate; keep yourself in the conversation.

Pouncing

This is when we try to ignore or eliminate the "other" in the online conflict. We pounce or blame another person as a way of driving him or her away from the disagreement. It's when we want the other person to placate. Flaming is the online equal of pouncing and is often based on the belief that my view is the only "right" one and on a dog-eat-dog assumption. Some signs of flaming are name calling, rejection, hostile questioning, hostile joking, and accusations. Flaming is an example of controlling an online conflict. It is unresponsive because it fails to acknowledge the other person's opinions. When someone flames, they tend to communicate with an air of superiority and intimidation. They can run the gamut from "deadly quiet" to sarcastic and "loud." Often they type in ALL CAPS, which is interpreted as yelling online. Pouncers—online flamers—are so intent on being right that they don't really read what other online students are writing, even when asked a direct question.

Don't pounce; invite other opinions into the conversation.

Distracting

Distracting is when we try to change the "subject" of the online conflict. It assumes that if you change the subject, the conflict will go away. It doesn't. The clearest sign of distracting is an abrupt change of topic. One example is when the online student substitutes "social chat" for substantive responses to discussion questions. This conflict usually centers on the person's role as an online student. Many people enter online learning programs expecting a "correspondence course" experience. Often what they find is a structured educational experience with required social interaction and expectations for contributing to the understanding of a subject matter. If an online student is not prepared for such a role (which is the conflict), he or she often responds with social chat or low participation. Other online students must recognize the distracting nature of this behavior and encourage the student to contribute by asking specific questions that will move the student forward. The conflict must be recognized—online students need to be prepared for angry responses when such a student is pushed to contribute. Such distracting is an example of diverting a real underlying conflict.

Don't distract—stick to the topic; politely ask other online students who are off the topic to explain how their comments relate to the subject at hand.

Computing

Computing is when we try to ignore the emotional climate of the online conflict. It is an example of not only ignoring the human potential of online learning, but further dehumanizing an online conflict. It is unresponsive because it fails to acknowledge the feelings of a real person on the other end of the computer. It sees the online environment as simply technical, not interpersonal. When someone computes, they tend to remain impersonal. They use jargon and technical language. Often they only want to deal with "the cold, hard facts." "Computers" are so intent on being detached that they often talk in the third person and show little awareness of audience and personal voice. Instead of seeing what others in the class are up to, and writing more as dialogue, they remain abstract.

Don't compute online; take people's feelings into consideration.

CONCLUSION

The most effective way to communicate through conflict is "responding." It is communication that "responds" to all four parts of the conflict—you, the other online student, the topic, and the electronic climate. It responds to feelings and "stands up for its own rights." It responds to the other student by asking about and listening for feelings and attitudes, and it "sticks to the topic." Finally, it responds to the emotional climate of the conflict by recognizing that feelings have a place online.

I end this chapter with some suggestions that can be directly applied to the online class. Responding effectively to online conflict can be practiced by using certain kinds of interpersonal and supportive statements, as detailed in the following list.

- *Use Descriptive Language:* Use nonevaluative statements about events and behaviors related to the conflict. For example, you might write a note to another student's personal mailbox where you say, "I feel that you were trying to be humorous with this statement, but it can come across as a bit sarcastic to some people. What do you think?" Offer your perspective while inviting the perspective of the other online student. Begin with a positive overture.

- *Set Personal Limits:* Try using statements that explicitly qualify the nature and extent of the conflict, and set clear personal boundaries. If another online student has been disruptive, don't take the bait. You might first make a comment in the main meeting about the strengths of the other student's opinions and then suggest alternative ways of seeing things. This step allows the other student to save face while you set important limits. The point is not to take it personally. Respect your own standards of integrity and don't get pulled into a flaming war. Keep your cool. Don't placate, but don't pounce!

- *Offer Support:* Make statements that express understanding, acceptance, or positive regard for the other person. Send messages to the main meeting telling other online students how much you appreciate the tone of their online communication. In this way, you help establish some cultural norms for the class. Be good listener, ask questions, focus on the arguments of your fellow students directly, and don't be defensive. This helps establish a positive emotional context for online communication.

- *Emphasize Commonalties and Relationship Reminders:* Statements that comment on common ground also help establish a productive tone for addressing conflict. Send a message to the main meeting saying something to this effect: "As a member of this class, I'm feeling uncomfortable with the tone of the present conversation. I'm feeling that some people could interpret it as sarcastic. What does everyone else feel?" In this message, you emphasize a common ground as members of the class and as human beings with feelings. It reminds online students that conflict exists within a broader context of mutual commitment, respect, human feelings, understanding, and learning. Emphasize a win-win solution.

- *Focus on the Problem, Not the Personality:* Initiate mutual consideration of solutions. If there is a conflict with another online student, attempt to describe the issue objectively and ask him or her how the problem can be solved. Use "I" statements that help you focus on the topic or issue, and not "you" statements that tend to focus on another's personality or character. It's your fellow online student's ideas or positions that you disagree with, not with his or her personality. Separate the people from the problem. Stick to the topic.

- *Defuse:* Ask yourself, "How well am I responding to conflict?" Defusing is identifying areas of agreement and maintaining a positive tone. By listening carefully and communicating your own values cautiously, you can help create a sense of openness and trust, and mutual respect for differences in the online classroom.

Finally, you can respond most effectively to online conflict by remembering that conflict is an important learning opportunity. I hope this chapter helps!

Conflict can show online students that they are "talking" with other people online who have feelings, thoughts, and lives of their own.

The Opportunity to Promote Online Decision Making

The "adversary system" of our courts operates on the assumption that truth and justice emerge from the clash of ideas. The above example also shows how the clash of ideas and disagreements can lead to more workable decisions in the online classroom. The online instructor was able to get Richard to "own" the decision to temper his communication because the conflict was posed as a problem in need of a solution, not a conflict in need of resolution. If the instructor's decision to stop all sharing of personal moral viewpoints had been imposed, Richard and other students would have felt "disenfranchised." They would have most certainly carried around increased feelings of isolation and resentments about the decision that could have interfered with future performance, cooperation, and decisions in the online classroom. The ultimate decision got the task completed and it strengthened relationships. In addition, Richard felt a part of the decision and was more likely to respect it. He realized that he was part of a real—though online—community.

The Opportunity to Help Students See That Feelings Exist Online

Here I must emphasize that I am not talking about allowing online students to flame each other. It's crucial that feelings are communicated productively online. I am talking about opportunities to express and explain feelings through respectful language. Online conflicts, if responded to effectively, can be positive opportunities for getting feelings out in a medium that is mostly assumed to be impersonal.

Dealing with feelings shows students the human element that is always present in the online environment.

As the example above shows, if the energy of a feeling like anger can be channeled into a positive communication framework, the feelings can be used to find creative solutions and more complete human relationships.

The Opportunity to Promote Confidence in Online Learning

There is always uncertainty in a person when things really get difficult. The first serious argument with another student is a major event. This is especially true in online learning situations where the phenomenon of flaming suggests that communication becomes more extreme and impulsive. But the confidence that follows a well-managed online conflict can be extremely valuable to learning. It is often those educational encounters that avoid conflict that are ultimately the most insecure and unproductive because they remain untested. Both online students in the above example felt a new sureness, a new security, in their working relationship. Their online relationship was tested by conflict, and they had the opportunity to develop trust and confidence by learning how to communicate successfully through those conflicts. They ultimately recognized the value of the experience and the important learning that took place.

Of course, a positive attitude is the first step to responding effectively to online conflict. Online students need to begin seeing conflict as creative and productive. The second step is to recognize that online conflict comes in several types.

TYPES OF ONLINE CONFLICT

Conflict is a pervasive part of all human relationships, including those in the online classroom. In order to respond effectively to online conflict, online students also need to recognize that not all disagreement is the same. There are three basic types of online conflict: over facts or interpretations, over online roles and identities, and over values.

Conflict over Facts or Interpretations

This kind of disagreement reflects differing views over the content and expectations of an online course. They are disagreements over fact. We can disagree over the fact that Columbus landed in the New World in 1492 (which we can easily confirm or disconfirm) or we can disagree over meaning—whether he "discovered" America at all (which is a matter of interpretation). The most important question to ask yourself when dealing with this type of online conflict is: What level of conflict are you disagreeing about—fact or meaning? It makes a difference. Your syllabus may say that you are required to interact in the online class, but what does "interaction" mean? If you are always responding to other student comments with short statements such as "I agree," are you actually interacting? And what is "correct" grammar online? Should online discussions be evaluated by the same grammatical standards as more formal online assignments like term papers or case studies? Or are online discussions, although textual, more like conversations? In addition, what does "page" mean online? Is a page one screen or is it a traditional page in length? These kinds of small conflicts over facts and interpretations can be very disruptive in an online class until they are discussed and clarified.

One fundamental online conflict over facts or interpretation can be about what an "online class" is. Generally speaking, an online course can be accessed anywhere and anytime and makes use of computer technology to deliver student learning at flexible times and places. But some online classes do not require any attendance or participation and resemble "correspondence courses" more than structured educational experiences that include interaction with faculty and other students, due dates, institutional support, and the kinds of materials that contribute to the development of a full course. Many online students enter programs with their own definition of what an online course is and there is an immediate need to clarify the nature of the course and the roles of faculty members and students.

Conflict over Online Roles and Identities

This kind of disagreement particularly reflects differing perspectives over the roles of online instructors. Cues in traditional educational settings reinforce social differences. An instructor lecturing at the front of a classroom or meeting a student in an office is a reminder of status differences. Online technologies weaken social differences apparent in face-to-face communication. Online instructors are not awarded authority or expertise by students simply because instructors look the part. All online messages have an equal status to a certain degree because they look alike. The only thing that can set them apart is their content, or what William James might call their "cash value." Without the "halo effect" of status, the competence and ability of the online instructor are in question from the beginning of class and are only earned through the quality of messages and how informative they are. While traditional students in a regular classroom might tend to accept the instructor's viewpoints as authority, online students tend to more readily question and challenge instructor opinions.

Consequently, many online conflicts about roles and identities focus on whether an instructor is considered informed or uninformed or are centered on who has what kind of authority with a given topic. Being labeled by students as informed is an important step in defining the position as the online instructor, but that is balanced against similar needs of many online students. Many online students are working adults in established careers. They have learned enormously from certain important work and other life experiences, as well as having formal education. They have learned how to learn a great deal in ways other than taking courses. They are the "experts" in many topics. This experience needs to be recognized and utilized by the online instructor. That's why many online instructors prefer to identify themselves as "facilitators" rather than instructors, understanding that online conflicts around power relationships can be understood as struggles over such identities and roles.

Conflict over Values

Effective online instructors recognize that online classes are part of social organizations as well as places where people accomplish individual and collective tasks. Over time, most organizations develop a culture that strongly affects the way people view their place of work, its management, and its primary purposes. Although culture in organizations is defined as the common values of both managers and employees, cultural values are not imposed. They are developed over time. There can be disagreements over organizational values, such as over the level of expectations of all members of the staff and regarding what service to customers means. In fact, conflict over cultural values may be necessary. Communication and human relations in organizations with well-defined, positive cultural values are nearly always better than in those that pay little attention to the values of the organization. There is value in communicating through conflict about organizational values. But they are most effectively dealt with in a structured way where there is an opportunity for mutual respect, for learning, and for maintaining interpersonal relationships.

As suggested above, the values of various online programs differ. For example, is "education" a value? It is clear that some working adults who enter online programs don't really want the education—they want what the education provides for them in better jobs, moving up the career ladder, and the ability to communicate ideas. But are those the values of the particular online programs they enter? If, as an online student, you enter your class with the above values but the instructor expects an "intellectual life," then there might be a conflict over values.

Ultimately, the main point is to know your conflict. Whatever the type of conflict, the next step in responding effectively is knowing what to do, or I should say knowing what not to do—reacting.

REACTING TO ONLINE CONFLICT

Going back to the beginning of this chapter and the distinction made between "reacting" and "responding," the following ways of dealing with online conflict can be identified as "reactive." A reactive approach does not see that whenever there is disagreement, there are always four elements to the conflict: (1) you, (2) the other person, (3) the topic, and (4) the climate.

The first three elements of conflict are easy to understand. The "you" of a conflict is all of us as we deal with the second part of conflict—"other" people. The topic, of course, is the subject of what we are talking about. On the other hand, the last element needs further explanation. The climate of a conflict can be the physical environment and objects (on the phone; face to face; in the kitchen, office, or bedroom; the temperature of the room; over the computer) but also the emotional level of the topic. For example, the emotional context of an online climate includes the lack of many nonverbals we have during face-to-face interaction.

Virginia Satir in *Peoplemaking* defines the reactive styles in these four ways: placating, pouncing, distracting, and computing.

Placating

Placating is when we ignore ourselves in online conflict. It is an example of denying that a conflict exists. It is unresponsive because it fails to acknowledge disagreement. It avoids the conflict by using statements that terminate "talk" about the conflict before the discussion has thoroughly developed. It writes in generalities and avoids specifics. When online students placate a conflict, they don't directly accept their responsibility. Often online placators "lurk" in the background of the class, simply observing and keeping their opinions to themselves.

Don't placate; keep yourself in the conversation.

Pouncing

This is when we try to ignore or eliminate the "other" in the online conflict. We pounce or blame another person as a way of driving him or her away from the disagreement. It's when we want the other person to placate. Flaming is the online equal of pouncing and is often based on the belief that my view is the only "right" one and on a dog-eat-dog assumption. Some signs of flaming are name calling, rejection, hostile questioning, hostile joking, and accusations. Flaming is an example of controlling an online conflict. It is unresponsive because it fails to acknowledge the other person's opinions. When someone flames, they tend to communicate with an air of superiority and intimidation. They can run the gamut from "deadly quiet" to sarcastic and "loud." Often they type in ALL CAPS, which is interpreted as yelling online. Pouncers—online flamers—are so intent on being right that they don't really read what other online students are writing, even when asked a direct question.

Don't pounce; invite other opinions into the conversation.

Distracting

Distracting is when we try to change the "subject" of the online conflict. It assumes that if you change the subject, the conflict will go away. It doesn't. The clearest sign of distracting is an abrupt change of topic. One example is when the online student substitutes "social chat" for substantive responses to discussion questions. This conflict usually centers on the person's role as an online student. Many people enter online learning programs expecting a "correspondence course" experience. Often what they find is a structured educational experience with required social interaction and expectations for contributing to the understanding of a subject matter. If an online student is not prepared for such a role (which is the conflict), he or she often responds with social chat or low participation. Other online students must recognize the distracting nature of this behavior and encourage the student to contribute by asking specific questions that will move the student forward. The conflict must be recognized—online students need to be prepared for angry responses when such a student is pushed to contribute. Such distracting is an example of diverting a real underlying conflict.

Don't distract—stick to the topic; politely ask other online students who are off the topic to explain how their comments relate to the subject at hand.

Computing

Computing is when we try to ignore the emotional climate of the online conflict. It is an example of not only ignoring the human potential of online learning, but further dehumanizing an online conflict. It is unresponsive because it fails to acknowledge the feelings of a real person on the other end of the computer. It sees the online environment as simply technical, not interpersonal. When someone computes, they tend to remain impersonal. They use jargon and technical language. Often they only want to deal with "the cold, hard facts." "Computers" are so intent on being detached that they often talk in the third person and show little awareness of audience and personal voice. Instead of seeing what others in the class are up to, and writing more as dialogue, they remain abstract.

Don't compute online; take people's feelings into consideration.

CONCLUSION

The most effective way to communicate through conflict is "responding." It is communication that "responds" to all four parts of the conflict—you, the other online student, the topic, and the electronic climate. It responds to feelings and "stands up for its own rights." It responds to the other student by asking about and listening for feelings and attitudes, and it "sticks to the topic." Finally, it responds to the emotional climate of the conflict by recognizing that feelings have a place online.

I end this chapter with some suggestions that can be directly applied to the online class. Responding effectively to online conflict can be practiced by using certain kinds of interpersonal and supportive statements, as detailed in the following list.

- *Use Descriptive Language:* Use nonevaluative statements about events and behaviors related to the conflict. For example, you might write a note to another student's personal mailbox where you say, "I feel that you were trying to be humorous with this statement, but it can come across as a bit sarcastic to some people. What do you think?" Offer your perspective while inviting the perspective of the other online student. Begin with a positive overture.
- *Set Personal Limits:* Try using statements that explicitly qualify the nature and extent of the conflict, and set clear personal boundaries. If another online student has been disruptive, don't take the bait. You might first make a comment in the main meeting about the strengths of the other student's opinions and then suggest alternative ways of seeing things. This step allows the other student to save face while you set important limits. The point is not to take it personally. Respect your own standards of integrity and don't get pulled into a flaming war. Keep your cool. Don't placate, but don't pounce!
- *Offer Support:* Make statements that express understanding, acceptance, or positive regard for the other person. Send messages to the main meeting telling other online students how much you appreciate the tone of their online communication. In this way, you help establish some cultural norms for the class. Be good listener, ask questions, focus on the arguments of your fellow students directly, and don't be defensive. This helps establish a positive emotional context for online communication.
- *Emphasize Commonalties and Relationship Reminders:* Statements that comment on common ground also help establish a productive tone for addressing conflict. Send a message to the main meeting saying something to this effect: "As a member of this class, I'm feeling uncomfortable with the tone of the present conversation. I'm feeling that some people could interpret it as sarcastic. What does everyone else feel?" In this message, you emphasize a common ground as members of the class and as human beings with feelings. It reminds online students that conflict exists within a broader context of mutual commitment, respect, human feelings, understanding, and learning. Emphasize a win-win solution.
- *Focus on the Problem, Not the Personality:* Initiate mutual consideration of solutions. If there is a conflict with another online student, attempt to describe the issue objectively and ask him or her how the problem can be solved. Use "I" statements that help you focus on the topic or issue, and not "you" statements that tend to focus on another's personality or character. It's your fellow online student's ideas or positions that you disagree with, not with his or her personality. Separate the people from the problem. Stick to the topic.

- ***Defuse:*** Ask yourself, "How well am I responding to conflict?" Defusing is identifying areas of agreement and maintaining a positive tone. By listening carefully and communicating your own values cautiously, you can help create a sense of openness and trust, and mutual respect for differences in the online classroom.

Finally, you can respond most effectively to online conflict by remembering that conflict is an important learning opportunity. I hope this chapter helps!

Identifying and Responding to an Online Conflict

In order to help you deal with online conflict effectively, use this checklist to evaluate your knowledge and skills about a specific conflict:

- What is the conflict about? Facts? Roles? Values?

  _____

  _____

  _____

- What is the emotional climate or context of this conflict?

  _____

  _____

  _____

- Are you listening with an open mind to what the other person has to say?

  _____

  _____

  _____

- Are you making your opinions known to the other person?

  _____

  _____

  _____

- Are you keeping your cool during any conflict and responding to the other student with respect and understanding? Would you be OK if you received your own messages?

_____

_____

_____

- Are you using descriptive language and setting personal limits?

_____

_____

_____

- How are you offering support? Emphasizing commonalties? Reminding the other person of your relationship as online learners?

_____

_____

_____

- Are you focusing on the topic and avoiding statements on the other person's personality? How are you defusing the conflict?

_____

_____

_____

CHAPTER 13

CONNECTING FOR SUCCESS IN THE ONLINE CLASSROOM

ROBERT H. WOODS, JR. AND SAMUEL EBERSOLE

In this chapter, you will learn about:

- How the online student can develop a social support structure
- Ways to make the online learning experience rich and enjoyable
- Online and offline tools to aid you in successfully integrating your academic and social environments

According to an online student in one of our classes, "the biggest void in this or any online program is the lack of a sense of community and the social aspect of attending class." Another student put it this way: "Sometimes it's hard to connect with other students in a meaningful way . . . by the time we get to know each other the semester is over." Still another student remarked, "instead of a number, I'm a screen name . . . that can be depressing at times . . . I just don't know how to connect or to be part of the class."

As a new online student, you may find that failure to address the relational concerns just noted may result in poor academic performance, greater feelings of isolation, and subsequent withdrawal from courses. More often than not, most students wait for the professor to do something that magically binds them with others in meaningful ways. While online facilitators can create meaningful opportunities for relationship building, successful online students take responsibility and manage their own social environments in proactive ways. Successful online students take advantage of certain online and offline strategies designed to connect them with other students and faculty.

In this chapter we'll propose and discuss several online and offline strategies we've used to connect online students with one another and with faculty. Students have told us that these strategies are extremely helpful in creating supportive communication environments, improving class performance, and enhancing their overall satisfaction with the online learning experience. We'll begin by introducing you to what we call *communal scaffolding*. Once the scaffolding concept has been explained, we provide a list of online and offline tools to aid you in successfully integrating your academic and social environments.

WHAT IS COMMUNAL SCAFFOLDING?

As Figure 13.1 depicts, communal scaffolding recognizes that successful online students must "build" social support if they are to maximize learning benefits. Scaffolding is commonly used in building construction to provide support for the structure, add an element of safety to the project, and provide

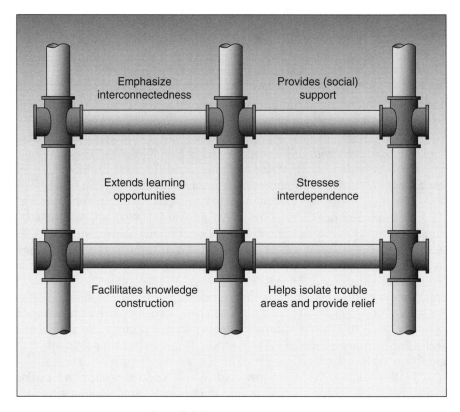

FIGURE 13.1   Communal scaffolding.

a secure place to stand for the workers. Similarly, communal scaffolding encourages and reinforces cognitive development in the context of social connection and facilitation. As interpersonal dynamics are fitted into the existing course and institutional structures—through various online and offline strategies—students are able to extend their range of learning opportunities by collaborating with others to achieve goals and complete assignments not otherwise possible. Finally, the scaffold helps instructors and others isolate individual student needs and customize communication to address a range of learning styles.

When we talk about communal scaffolding in this context, we are referring to bridging the gap between the task (cognitive, intellectual) and interpersonal (social, interpersonal) requirements of online learning.

Overall, the communal scaffold concept should help you better conceptualize the interconnectedness and interdependence that is so necessary for successful online learning. It demonstrates how you, as an online student, can take responsibility for building social support and other collaborative structures alongside course facilitators. The scaffold lets instructors visualize how optimal online learning may require that certain instructional strategies or mechanisms be condensed, adjusted, reorganized, or eliminated as participants in the learning experience construct an understanding of theories and applications.

By now you have already realized that successful online learning requires more than just the transfer of knowledge from Point A (instructor) to Point B (student). A dynamic comes into play when online students are empowered to participate in the learning process. As we build an online learning community together, we must take advantage of all the tools at our disposal—tools that have both technological and social dimensions.

The issue then is whether the scaffold you construct is sufficient to support your desired online learning outcomes. Scaffolding and learning outcomes are directly related. Students and faculty intentionally construct interpersonal intimacy and community through multiple modes of online and offline communication tools. These tools significantly impact student motivation, performance, personal growth, harmony, inclusiveness, and satisfaction in the online learning experience. Figure 13.2 more clearly demonstrates the central role that communal scaffolding plays in linking course objectives, assignments, and learning outcomes with social support and your needs as an online student.

The next two sections turn our attention to several communication tools that will help you construct your communal scaffold. You can scaffold *online* using personalized email, personal discussion folders, immediacy, audio/video, and live chat, to name a few. You scaffold *offline* through field trips, road trips, on-site experiences, internships, apprenticeships, service learning, cohort group meetings, and phone calls.

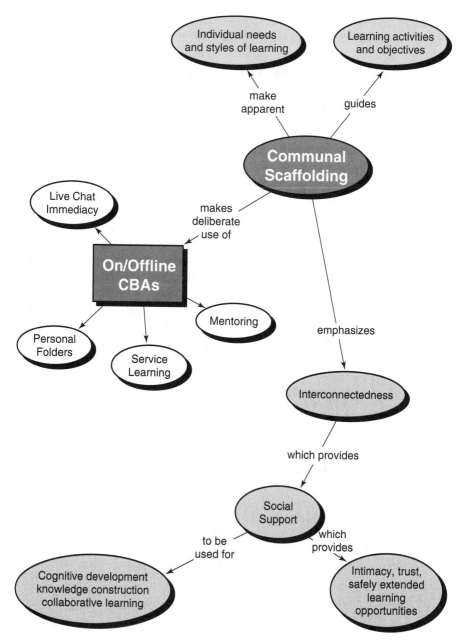

FIGURE 13.2 Use of communal scaffolding in linking elements of online learning.

ONLINE STRATEGIES FOR COMMUNAL SCAFFOLDING

Here are several online strategies students have used in our classes to connect with their fellow students and faculty. We call these basic strategies and communication tools community building activities (CBAs). They are reliable strategies that are common in most online learning environments, and are easy to incorporate without being intimidating. They produce immediate, observable benefits as well as long-term change in the social environment.

Personal Discussion Folders

Most course platforms incorporate some form of personal, nonsubject-matter-specific "discussion boards," often referred to as discussion "folders," "rooms," or "forums." These are simply gathering places where personalized exchanges between participants in online courses may occur. Most online instructors create folders titled "Autobiographies," "Introductions," "Icebreakers," or "Name and Face," where your "e-personality" can be posted and disclosed. Personal introductions of this sort usually occur during the first several days of class before you begin discussing course content. The benefits of self-disclosure extend to the larger issue of group or class dynamics. The more accurate information you provide to the larger group at this stage, the less potential for the negative effects of "anonymity" in other course areas later. Most students consider their personality to function as an "online passport." If possible, complete the passport effect by including a personal photograph. We've found that students report feeling closer or more connected to other students in the course when they can see their photographs. This is one of the reasons that we include our personal photographs as part of the faculty homepage.

We also encourage you to use other personal discussion folders as they appear—even if they aren't required. This may include anything from a folder titled "Virtual Cafe" to one titled "Meditations" or "Thoughts of the Day." In any case, your participation in these folders communicates your commitment to the learning experience and willingness to get to know others. Participating in these folders may even help you reinforce or maintain relationships previously established in the Autobiographies or Introduction folder. If you don't see any folders of this kind, don't hesitate to ask your instructor to set some up. We've always been willing to set up folders based on student recommendations. Even professors can't read minds and we don't always think of everything—contrary to what you might believe!

Immediacy

To give your classmates the impression that you are "present" with them, respond to email or threaded discussion in a timely manner. One student captured this idea when he said, "every time I log back on to Blackboard, usually the next day, same time, I always see a response . . . it's as if I never left the day before, like our communication is simultaneous . . . almost like we're having a 'real' conversation." As a rule, we suggest responding to one another's communication within 24 hours.

We also recommend using the other person's first name in your reply to create greater interpersonal awareness. Some students refer back to a contribution in a former post to connect the past with the immediate present. Students have commented that, as instructors, we "seem to never leave!" Although it feels like we sometimes live online—or at least that's what our spouses tell us—we actually do leave. I think we create the impression of never leaving by making several postings in each course area every time we log on. Other students perceive students who are very active in one course area but absent from another as less present in the course as a whole. Therefore, even if you are just checking in to catch up on the day's postings, stop by one or more of the rooms and let your presence be known in some way, shape, or form. Consider it akin to simply "showing up" for an on-campus course.

Live Chat

If "virtual office" hours are available through an online chat function, we recommend that you schedule at least one appointment with your instructor. Students tell us that live chat of this kind helps them connect with us— at a safer distance than a phone call—early on in the semester in ways that email or voicemail cannot. Live chat also lets you have a conversation with your instructor without paying for a long-distance call. These chats can even be archived and reviewed by others in the class at a later time. Students who cannot make it to the virtual hours can still benefit from the questions asked by others. Just as in real-time office sessions, live chats let you engage in more informal, personal interaction with your instructor than formal group discussion usually allows.

We recognize that you, as an online student, might not be making the choice whether live chat will be implemented within a particular course for virtual office hours or class discussion purposes. Most Web-based educational platforms now come equipped with a live chat option built into course communication that students can use with relative ease. As a student, you might want to suggest to the facilitator or other online students that you interact via live chat on a regular or semi-regular basis about course content or procedures. Upon hearing this request, most instructors will take the initiative to set up regular time for live chat. If your course management platform does not include this function, you can always use something like Instant Messaging (IM). Video conferencing programs, such as NetMeeting, allow the incorporation of video and audio elements simultaneously.

We've observed that students seeking stronger connections will schedule live chat with other students in one of the personalized discussion rooms (for example, Autobiographies or Virtual Cafe). Our experience tells us that more so than any other CBA, live chats enable students to be more immediate with other students and instructors. Students tell us that their experiences with other students and instructors are more intimate—that is, less distant—than other mediated exchanges. One student reported that live chat takes connectedness to the "next level." Not everyone uses this option, so don't feel slighted if your instructor or other students don't engage in live chat. In our experience, those who participate in these chats are more active in required class discussion and report higher levels of satisfaction with learning online than those who do not use live chat functions.

Personalized Email

Another way to connect with online faculty and other students is to send personalized email (PE) outside of regular class time or required course discussion. Personalized email might be used to encourage a fellow student who made a solid contribution in one of the required discussion formats. Most PEs are typically two to three sentences long (between 40 and 50 words on average) and include general words of encouragement, caring, or support. For example, if another student articulates something that you have been struggling with, you might compliment that student's reflection and critical thinking. You can also use PEs to check up on someone who doesn't appear to be as active in discussions as others. Something like "haven't seen you in discussion for awhile . . . miss your contribution . . . hope all is well" seems to reestablish contact with someone who might feel marginalized. Depending on the size of the class and your time, you can send the same type of personalized emails to small groups. Student replies to PEs sent by other students as well as by us indicate that most perceive these contacts as "invitations to socialize," or to go to a "deeper level," much as an invitation to have a drink or a cup of coffee after class might accomplish. Colleagues see students who send PEs as caring, supportive, and trustworthy. Two or three well-timed PEs can set off a domino effect and create a strong, long-lasting social support network within a relatively short period of time.

Audio/Video

Some online learners and instructors send audio messages as a supplement to text, and as email attachments to build relationships with fellow online learners. A variation of the audio message as email attachment is the PowerPoint slide with recorded narration. To this, others have added personal photographs or other graphics. As audio experimenters ourselves, we've found that our tone of voice can be used to set the right mood for future communication. It becomes a perceptual framework through which subsequent communication is filtered. The tone of an audio message sent just before an exam or final paper to another student can even help reduce anxieties. All you need is a microphone and a plug-in such as RealProducer, which is a free download on the Web. Windows Media Player (available on most PCs) can also be used.

With the growth of easy-to-use video production tools, some daring souls have ventured into "video welcomes" or introductions. We typically include a 30-second video welcome as part of our faculty pages. I do this using a standard DV camera and a basic video capture program that compresses and saves the file in a manageable size. You can do the same as part of your class introduction (in the Autobiographies folder) or on your personal home page (most Web-based platforms, such as Blackboard, allow you to create your very own home page). Video is slightly more sophisticated, but not beyond your reach. If you have the skills and tools to produce video, then go for it. If not, we recommend that you do not take time away from other CBAs to learn how to produce video. A PowerPoint slide with your picture and recorded narration can accomplish a similar effect until you have more time to learn how to produce your own video. We've found that students who need the "extra touch" that audio or video elements provide report feeling closer to others after hearing their voices. It somehow humanizes what would be an otherwise isolated experience for some in ways that other CBAs cannot.

Private Places

This might sound strange at first blush, but to the extent allowable by the instructor and course management platform, create a separate private area for you and your assigned discussion group apart from general class discussion. In Blackboard, we usually create a "cyber study room" where previously assigned discussion groups can meet apart from required discussion formats for informal chat or threaded discussion. This is the same idea as the personal discussion folders mentioned earlier, but for individual groups only. This is a space that the instructor may not enter unless invited. It is a group "safe haven." Members of other discussion groups cannot enter or view the communication that occurs in this room either. If the class is small (10 or fewer students) and consists of only one group, then the personal discussion folders might be used for the same purpose.

Regular Updates

Everyone likes to see fresh, new content, which is an important indication that value is constantly being added to your learning experience. As instructors, we send weekly updates to students related to course content and procedures. Some students adopt a similar model, and send brief weekly updates to us about their progress on group projects and theses. One student titled her update "What's new with Sarah . . .?" Some students use regular updates to help them figure out whether they are "on the right track." In this sense, these updates function as a perceptual check of sorts to help students assess individual progress in a given course. For instance, if you are struggling with certain course content, send an update in bullet format to your instructor for feedback. You can do this on a regular or semi-regular basis. Ask the instructor how well you understand the material based on your update. As mentioned earlier (see "Audio/Video"), if you include the update on a PowerPoint slide, you can add audio narration with little hassle. The more detail you can provide, the better, but make sure you don't overwhelm the instructor with too many slides. As a general rule, we don't mind reviewing 3–5 slides sent by a student needing clarification or special assistance.

Group Discussion and Style

Last, but certainly not least, one of the most basic but often most underestimated online strategies you can use to build connectedness revolves around participation in required group discussion formats. Woody Allen is quoted as having once said, "90 percent of life is just showing up." For most things that may be true, and to some extent we can apply this to your participation in the online setting. But just "showing up" will only get you halfway toward your desired goal. In addition, your *discursive* or writing style in online discussion may prevent you from connecting with others. As mentioned in earlier chapters, online students desire both interpersonal interaction and a safe learning environment that welcomes alternative or opposing views. Thus, while it's all right to critically challenge ideas, watch that you avoid accusatory language or leading questions that indicate your biases. Nothing seems to kill a feeling of belonging or togetherness faster. Instead, use concrete and descriptive language in your replies. Remember to encourage and model personal expression, whether through nicknames, emoticons, or other types of interpersonal communication. Always begin your reply to another's post with a positive comment before critically addressing other matters. Threaded dialogue can lay a foundation for a more elaborate communal structure. Feeling "safe" to express one's views is an important part of building community.

OFFLINE STRATEGIES FOR COMMUNAL SCAFFOLDING

Now that online strategies for constructing your scaffold have been explored, we'll explore several offline strategies. Offline efforts to build community, when carefully integrated with the learning objectives of the course, can greatly enhance students' experiences.

Although much of the recent research has been exploring ways to improve online communication, it is almost always undertaken with the assumption that online communication begins at a disadvantage to offline, or face-to-face (F2F), communication. We need to point out that by F2F we don't necessarily mean traditional, passive lecture presentations. F2F should be much more than that, and should precipitate the kind of active participation and interactivity that is also the goal for online communication. *Interactivity* should also be understood in terms of both interaction with the course content and interaction with students and instructors.

Following are several offline strategies, or offline CBAs, that can be employed to encourage and enhance the building and strengthening of relationships. Note that even though most of these CBAs can best be initiated and implemented by the instructor, they can also be incorporated by students.

Field Trips

If possible, think of a reason to take your class "on the road." By this we mean find an opportunity to suggest a visit to a site where there is opportunity for practical application of the classroom theory. Recently, we joined a small group of students traveling to a fairly distant city for a daylong seminar that was being sponsored by a professional organization. The experience of overcoming a common adversity (in this case, meeting at 5:45 A.M. in order to get to the seminar by 8 A.M.) and the camaraderie experienced during the 2-hour drive contributed to the development of relationships. The experience of sharing a meal on the trip home was another opportunity for relationships to be strengthened. Learning experiences from the road trip can later be incorporated in a classroom or online discussion. Specific course areas may even be created to provide a summary of attendees' experiences.

Students who live outside the instructor's geographic region—usual for most online students—can initiate a variation of this offline CBA. Students can meet a faculty member or other students at a conference or professional organization. We notify our students when we will be at a conference in their location, and tell them that we would like to get together for lunch or have them join us at the conference. Some out-of-state students even take the initiative to contact us when they will be in our area for a professional or personal engagement. We go out of our way in those cases to make the face-to-face meeting happen.

Internships and Service Learning

Seek out opportunities for internships, apprenticeship, and service learning. These offline strategies provide opportunities for online students to engage in experiential learning while they build relationships with people outside the traditional classroom. The relationships that are formed with colleagues, professionals, and members of the community not only have value from the perspective of networking, but they can be important connections to the kind of real-world experiences that students need. Students engaged in community projects or working side-by-side with professionals frequently find the human connection that allows them to connect theory and practice in ways that didn't make sense before. Service learning is practical application of knowledge and learning by working on community-based projects. Frequently associated with volunteer service projects, service learning allows student participants to practice interpersonal relationships and caring for others. You might apply your skills and training to solve a problem that might otherwise remain unsolved, and in so doing forge friendships and relationships that enrich your lives.

Cohort Groups and Projects

Some programs use this strategy during the summer prior to the first fall semester of classes. For example, online students might meet face-to-face on campus for an intensive two-to-three-week class session in early August. Individuals are assigned to small groups on the basis of personality inventories administered shortly after enrollment into the program. Students share meals, attend conferences, work on group assignments, and attend classes together. Students feel a strong sense of community with others following such meetings. Cohort activities greatly increase retention rates and reports of overall enjoyment with later online learning.

Another variation of this strategy is a cohort or class meeting within an individual class. In one instance, we held a class meeting halfway through the semester at a local coffeehouse. Students in the immediate area, and some as far as two to three hours away, attended the meeting. Upon return to our regularly scheduled online activities, we observed a measurable change in the depth of reflection in posts/replies to our discussion questions. We had fewer late papers and "absences." However, it is recommended that any such meeting take place only after students have demonstrated a certain level of comfort and responsibility in interacting with one another in the online setting.

Phone Calls

Although this may seem simplistic or obvious to some, online instructors and students often overlook it. It is surprising what a personal phone call can do to enhance a sense of connectedness. While the phone might arguably be seen as an online strategy, especially in light of emerging Internet phone services, and since it is more personal, more familiar, and less technologically complex than computer-mediated communication, we've chosen to treat it as an offline strategy. Besides, regardless of the originator's source, those on the receiving end will most always be using a traditional hand-held unit. And because phones are important social tools that are part of the American fabric, communication by phone is often perceived as less task-related than, say, email.

Recently, we took time to call all the students in a small upper-division class that I was teaching. I told the students that I was just calling to check in with them—that I didn't really have any particular information to pass along—but that I just wanted to let them know that I was available if they needed any help with the class. The response was extremely positive. We also called each of our online students in one master's-level course. A student had suggested that calling might "bring us closer together as a class, faster." He personally felt that receiving a phone call from us would make up for the "loss" he felt not being face to face. Nearly every student commented on the positive benefits of this phone call at some point before the end of the semester.

CONCLUSION

So, how do we encourage active engagement on the part of teachers and students, and how do we contribute to the kind of communal infrastructure that makes learning fun and exciting? Perhaps the final answer resides in some of the key indicators of community. Following this chapter is a checklist of such indicators. We encourage you to use the checklist to evaluate your online class. If most of these are present, it is a good indication that your communal scaffold is a strong one, and that you are well on your way to experiencing a rich learning community. There are no shortcuts to developing community. It takes time. But the time spent with classmates and with the instructor can be structured in such a way to facilitate the all-important transfer of intellectual and emotional capital.

■ ■ ■ ■ ■

Checklist of Connecting Skills

In order to help you create an online support structure, use this checklist to evaluate your online class.

- Do you know one another's names? _____ Yes _____ No

- Are you comfortable engaging classmates and instructors in conversation? _____ Yes _____ No

- Does the conversation extend outside the traditional instructional context? _____ Yes _____ No

- Do you share common goals and aspirations? _____ Yes _____ No

- Is there a sense that the "classroom" provides a safe environment for exploration and discovery? _____ Yes _____ No

- Are the learning outcomes ones that make sense to you and can you relate to them on a personal level? _____ Yes _____ No

- Have both students and teacher made an emotional commitment to the course? _____ Yes _____ No

- Is there a sense of shared responsibility? _____ Yes _____ No

CHAPTER 14

ONLINE MATHEMATICS COURSES

JEFFREY CRABILL

In this chapter, you will learn about:

- How to be successful in online mathematics classes
- Preparation for the course and a little bit of math psychology

So you have decided to take a math or statistics class online. Bravo! You are about to experience the flexibility that distance learning offers students. Sometimes in the classroom, we tend to let ourselves believe that the teacher is all knowing and all powerful. At the end of the term, we realize that the information just doesn't soak in and that if had we done the work from the beginning, success would have been ours.

Math is a very new subject for distance learning. Just a few years ago, no one ever imagined that math could be taught without a classroom. We still tend to believe that math can only be learned with lectures. In this chapter, I will discuss how to get over the stereotypical math class. Once we get past our preconceived ideas of how a math class should be, we can then talk about succeeding in distance learning. This can take a while and it will be your first big hurdle toward success in your online math class.

And remember that your goal is success! Pep rallies and cheers are given for football teams, so why not give yourself some of that spirit?

We'll begin by talking about preparation for the course and a little bit of math psychology. These are important things to understand when taking any mathematics course in any format. Once we are beyond that, I will discuss taking the mathematics course itself. You will find that much of this chapter is applicable to a traditional classroom course, and it is my intent for it to be a guide in that situation as well. But if you think about it, preparation, mindset, commitment, and hard work can achieve success in any course!

PREPARATION

Of all the things that we will discuss in this chapter, preparation is the most important item to consider when taking any math class. In my experience, math is the only subject that college students consider enrolling in for which they are unprepared. Have you ever heard yourself saying, "Well, I'll just get a tutor" or "I can do it if I just study more"? Needless to say, you must take some time either to properly place yourself in a course, or to have someone make a professional judgment as to which math course is best for you.

The first thing to do is to list the courses you have taken previously. Start with math courses you took in high school and write down the name of semester, the course name, and the grade you received. (Take the time to fill in the chart at the end of this chapter.)

Different schools generally offer math courses in a similar order, which is typically arithmetic, pre-algebra, beginning algebra, intermediate algebra, college algebra, pre-calculus, calculus, and beyond. Your school may have different names for these courses, so check with the math department to see what they are called.

Take a look at the chart you filled in and check with an advisor at your school to make sure that you meet the minimum prerequisites to take your online course. You are not saving yourself any time if you enroll in a course for which you are not prepared. Look very carefully at the grades you earned and the time that has passed since each course, and discuss with your advisor whether you are indeed prepared for your online course. Generally, if it has been more than a year since your last math course, you will want to be conservative in your placement.

Once you have written down your courses, it is time to see the online math department at your school. Most departments offer some sort of a placement test for new or returning students that will give you a sense of what you know and what you don't know. Take the results of this test to a math instructor or to a counselor, and have a frank discussion about the results. Teachers and counselors have quite a bit of experience placing new students in the right course, so take advantage of what they know. (Some schools may not give you a choice of courses since they may require you to take the course into which the exam placed you.)

If you want to take a placement test on your own, there are several resources available to you online. Arizona State University has a wonderful online placement test that will give you an idea of which course you should take. This page can be found at *http://fym.la.asu.edu/placement*. Here is a list of several other Web sites where information on placement can be obtained:

- *http://www.ku.edu/~advising/math/test.shtml (College Algebra)*
- *http://spot.pcc.edu/academ/math/placement/*

- *http://www.sosmath.com/cyberexam/cyber.html*
- *http://www.math.virginia.edu*
- *http://www.math.unl.edu/?area=MathPlacement*

Finally, remember that you are never doing yourself any favors by attempting to save yourself time when enrolling in a math class. Give yourself the proper skills before you enroll in any course. No one would take third-year French without a full second-year course! The same is true with math courses, so make sure that you have met all the necessary prerequisites for the course you wish you take.

A BIT OF MATH PSYCHOLOGY

Being a math teacher is very interesting. Almost every student I see starts a conversation with me by saying, "I have never really been very good at math, but . . ." If you have never said that to anyone, then maybe you once blamed your dislike of math on some previous teacher. Now that we're all admitting to something (and yes, I have done that as well!), we can get started.

Everyone in the world has had at least one success with math. Most of you may not even realize it. Math is so present in our daily lives that we tend to overlook it. Have you ever doubled a recipe for a party? Have you ever painted a room and estimated how many gallons of paint to buy? Do you go to the store and think about how much that shirt will cost after the clerk gives you that 40 percent discount? At a gas station, do you look at the number of gallons of gas you just bought to get a sense for your car's fuel economy?

These are just a few things that most people do regularly without knowing it. I'm not saying that you can figure out the price of that shirt to the penny, but I bet that you can get in the neighborhood. *That makes you good at math!* We are our own worst critics in life, and we spend countless hours beating ourselves down or trying to find someone to serve as a good scapegoat. My advice is *stop*! When you enter an online math classroom and tell yourself that you are bad at math, you have already done damage. I have often compared it to verbal abuse, except in this case you are abusing yourself.

STARTING YOUR ONLINE MATH CLASS

It is now time to begin the course. You are ready to take on the challenge of an online math course. Keep in mind that you are now in charge of your learning and learning is now on your terms. That is the exciting thing about learning mathematics online. You control how you learn and you can take advantage of what the online course has to offer you.

The most important part of your course is your online instructor. This person is your contact for all your questions and concerns. He or she has probably taught many students like you, so remember that your instructor knows what students need to learn. Don't be afraid of asking questions or even making constructive comments to your instructor. So many students have convinced themselves that math instructors are unapproachable, and true as that may sometimes be, half the responsibility lies with you—the student—to help create a good rapport between student and instructor.

From a technology standpoint, taking an English course online is easier than taking a math course. Modern computers are all outfitted with word processors that can handle essays and papers, but computers don't necessarily have programs that can handle mathematical symbols. You are probably very used to writing all your mathematics by hand, and probably haven't even thought of using a computer to type your math homework. In order to communicate via email with your instructor or other students, you will need a word processor that is able to create and format mathematical equations. For many years, I used Microsoft Word's Equation Editor. Your version of Word probably has Equation Editor already installed. This program allows you to create everything from fractions to exponents. I currently use Math Type (which must be purchased separately), which is another program that lets you create mathematical equations in a Word document. Other brands of word processors also have similar mathematical symbols available; click "help" to see what your word processor can do for you.

Now that you have a word processor capable of formatting mathematical symbols, you will want to communicate regularly with your instructor. Include in your emails examples of your work so that your instructor can help you find your mistakes and get on track again. If you take the time to type problems, your instructor will be much better able to help you.

Every online math course I have taught is built around a piece of interactive software. Examples of this software include Prentice Hall's *Interactive Math* and *Math Pro 5*, Brooks-Cole's *The Learning Equation*, or McGraw-Hill's *ALEKS*. I won't be discussing the pros and cons of each program, but these programs often are the core of an online course. Your instructor will expect that you make use of these programs to learn the material of the course, do your daily homework exercises, and possibly even take your exams.

Online math courses can have different formats as well. Many instructors will post daily or weekly notes that explain the current material. Success in this environment requires a lot of work on your part. First, download the instructor's information as soon as it is posted. Set aside a session when you can review the instructor's notes and put them into your own words. Working with other students to decipher the material may also make the process easier. This way, you can bounce thoughts and ideas around your study group.

Hopefully, you have learned enough material to do some review exercises. Do your assigned problems, but also consider checking another textbook out of the library and doing exercises in that book as well. Other textbooks (or Internet resources) may give you explanations or examples that are easier to understand. Your understanding of the material will be greatly improved if you have more than one source of information. Go to your library or search the Internet for extra information.

In the next section, I outline what a good student notebook can look like. When you are not in a classroom everyday, it is easy to slide on organization and homework. When you are going through your daily online lessons, you will need to put forth as much effort, if not more, than a classroom student does. Make a room of your home into a classroom, and adopt the same strategies for note taking and learning there as you would in a classroom.

CAN I REALLY LEARN MATH WITHOUT SEEING AN INSTRUCTOR?

This is not really a fair question because online learning changes everyone's role—both the student and the teacher! You have chosen to take your math course online and it can be very easy to forget about your instructor. But you do have an instructor, with whom you should communicate regularly, however your learning is delivered in this brand new way. The biggest hurdle—for both instructors and students—is to realize that learning takes place even if no one is lecturing. This is a huge change in thought that is happening right now. You have to get on board to succeed in your course.

Your instructor will naturally build some structure into your online math course, but you will have to create some of your own. I compare this to the production of a major stage play. The actors have daily rehearsals, during which they practice their performances. This daily routine locks the information into each actor's mind and when the curtain rises on opening night, a flawless performance is given. Just like that actor, you need a daily rehearsal, or routine, and you get to be the actor and the director!

First, you need a good notebook that you dedicate entirely to your math class. Choose a 1½- to 2-inch three-ring binder with dividers. Get one notebook for each class because physical separation of notes and work supports the organization of the information you have in your mind.

I encourage my students to create sections in their notebooks called *Syllabus/Handouts*, *Notes*, *Homework*, *Journal*, and *Graded Work*.

The Syllabus Section

Here you should keep a copy of all the important paperwork that your instructor provides. All courses have a structured syllabus and this will be made available to you either on paper or on the Internet. If your instructor has your course syllabus on the Internet, *print* a copy and place it into this section of your notebook, along with a list of homework assignments, daily activities, and any other important material provided by your instructor. Highlight key information on your syllabus, such as exam dates, grading standards, the instructor's email address and telephone number, and any important course policies.

The Notes Section

This section should contain all the information you write down each day when you are working on your coursework. Many students forget the importance of taking notes when they are not copying them from an instructor. Just like in the traditional classroom, you will need to write down important pieces of information—formulas, procedures, and examples. I typically give my online students nongraded "practice" problems to be done before beginning the daily homework assignment, and I expect these problems to be in their *Notes* sections. How you organize your notes is up to you, but keep in mind that your notes are an extension of your memory, and you will have to refer to them later when studying for exams. At the very least, allow one page of notes per topic. This will keep your notes from being confusing and hard to use.

The Homework Section

The homework section of your notebook should contain each homework assignment that you have done during the semester. Students have a preferred way of formatting their homework. Some students like to fold their papers in half and others like to squish as many problems onto one page as possible. In my experiences, successful students are the ones who use lots of white space, and keep the number of problems per page to a minimum. In algebra courses, I encourage students to divide each sheet of paper into two columns and three rows. Each of the six boxes is usually just about enough space to complete one problem. You might want to consider two rows if you have larger handwriting. My point is that organization of your homework problems gives you a definite advantage when it comes to studying later on.

Raid recycle bins for extra paper so you won't have to worry about wasting a resource.

I believe that it is very important to keep track of the time you have spent and the work that you have done for any course that you take. Our time is our most valuable asset.

The Journal Section

This section of your notebook is for keeping a record of what you have done. Figure 14.1 shows what a typical daily entry can look like. I have found that this section of the notebook is the one that I examine most carefully when students come to ask me questions. I encourage students to keep track of the time that they spend on each section of the course so that they have an idea of the time necessary to learn something new. Students who do well in my courses are generally those who put in the proper amount of time each day, and who consistently ask me questions. Since your online course doesn't give you daily physical interaction with the instructor, this is a place where you can jot down your questions. When you call or email your instructor, you need only open your notebook to the journal and you'll have all your questions in one place.

DATE	START TIME	END TIME	SECTION WORKED	QUESTIONS REMAINING
9/30	10:00 A.M.	12:15 P.M.	3.3, started 3.4	How do I find the slope of a line with just two points?
Weekly Totals				Questions STILL remaining this week?

FIGURE 14.1   Typical entry to daily journal.

The Graded Work Section

In the back of your notebook, keep your graded work. Any work that is returned to you should go in this section. You may also want to keep a copy of the assignments that you have turned in to your instructor. Online learning sometimes requires you to mail or fax assignments, so you want to have copies in case something gets lost.

CONCLUSION

Remember that online mathematics is not for everyone. You must take some time to determine if you are the right type of student for an online course, using the information other contributors and I have presented in this book, along with a frank discussion with your instructor. If you decide that online learning is right for you, then you will have taken a first step into a larger world. This experience will make you a better student. You will become more independent and learn how to efficiently seek information on your own.

In addition, if you spend time with your math textbook, you may find it is easier to read than you previously believed. Math textbooks may not be as "Greek" as you once thought. If you learn to read them properly, textbooks can be a great part of your learning experience.

Most importantly, though, you will discover how you learn best. No two students learn in exactly the same way, and online learning—of any subject—provides you with the opportunity to learn most efficiently. You can adapt the course to your own style, rather than having to adjust to an instructor. The experience can give you more information about yourself than you may have had before, and hopefully you will be able to apply it to the rest of your education.

Good luck in your online math course. I really think that you will enjoy the experience.

Preparing for Your Online Math Course

In order to help you become an effective online math student, use this chart. Start with math courses you took in high school and write down the name of semester, the course name, and the grade you received:

SEMESTER AND YEAR	COURSE NAME	GRADE EARNED
High School		
9th grade	_____	_____
10th grade	_____	_____
11th grade	_____	_____
12th grade	_____	_____
College	_____	_____
	_____	_____
	_____	_____
	_____	_____
	_____	_____

Daily Journal for Your Online Math Course

In order to help you become an effective online math student, use this chart to keep track of your daily online math activities.

DATE	START TIME	END TIME	SECTION WORKED	QUESTIONS REMAINING
9/30	10:00 A.M.	12:15 P.M.	3.3, started 3.4	How do I find the slope of a line with just two points?
Weekly Totals				Questions STILL remaining this week?

■ ■ ■ ■ ■ ▬▬▬▬▬▬▬▬▬▬▬▬▬▬▬▬▬▬▬▬▬▬▬

STUDYING IN THE
ONLINE LIBRARY

RITA BARSUN

In this chapter, you will learn about:

- How you can benefit from an online library
- The types of online library services
- Suggestions for using online libraries effectively
- Questions to ask about online library services
- How to evaluate an online resource

Working closely with new students in the virtual academic environment has given me insight into their apprehensions about distance education, and expectations about online library services and resources. This chapter will help you understand what you can expect from your distance education institution, and how you can benefit from online library services and resources.

RESOURCES IN THE ONLINE LIBRARY

Most institutions that offer courses at a distance have invested great sums to provide their students with scholarly online databases. The contents of such databases have been carefully assembled and indexed by individuals familiar with the literature—the important books, journals, and other documents—of a particular academic discipline. Having access to them is vital to your online course work. The center of any virtual library is a collection of such databases. Although some databases contain only citations and abstracts for the books and articles you need in order to write papers or to do other course work, others contain the full text in digitized form.

The databases appear on the World Wide Web and are generally not available to the general public. Only those affiliated with the college or university that has paid a hefty subscription fee have access. As an online student, you access databases by supplying a username and password that you are given when you enroll. The databases are accessible 24 hours a day, seven days a week, so you can search them at your convenience. You can sit comfortably at home and "visit" the online library late at night, or at times when going out in the weather would be extremely unpleasant. You need not worry about the virtual library being closed for a holiday, although there may be brief periods during which the databases undergo maintenance and are temporarily offline. Online databases offer you the option of printing the materials, emailing them to yourself, or downloading to a disk or hard drive.

Searching online databases is an acquired skill, so librarians put effort into developing guides and tutorials to help you master the skill. Because the guides and tutorials are on the virtual library's Web site, you can access them at your leisure or when you have specific questions about how to look for information in a database. Some tutorials are interactive, requiring you to use your mouse or keyboard, while others present only instructions and illustrations.

Among the favorite resources of distance learners are electronic journals. Subscriptions to them are often too expensive for individuals, especially if the journals are scholarly or scientific in nature. Online librarians and faculty confer on which journals are key for the various programs of study and try to ensure that they are made available to students. You can search the online journals for key words, phrases, or names of persons. You can also browse the online table of contents for each issue to locate relevant articles.

Some virtual libraries have a reserve collection consisting of copies of journal articles and book chapters that have been selected by faculty for particular courses, electronically scanned, and mounted on a password-protected Web site. You can read the material online or print it. In some cases, you can download it or email it to yourself.

It is important to realize that the Web often falls short when it comes to support for online course work. The Web is not a library. First, a very small proportion of the world's print resources, especially scholarly documents, have been digitized and made available to the public. Second, much of what is on the Web is not reliable. Anyone with a computer and a basic knowledge of HTML coding can publish anything from nonsense to outright propaganda or lies. Third, even well-constructed search engines cannot find some of the best and most relevant material for your paper or research.

On the other hand, an online library can have a collection of links to scholarly or informational Web sites that the librarians have ferreted out. Typically, the informational sites are encyclopedias, dictionaries or thesauruses, writing guides, books of quotations, and other reference works. If the scholarly links are related to specific areas of study, they are carefully reviewed and selected by a faculty member and librarian with expertise in that field. They may include background information, the home pages of professional organizations, or some electronic journals that are publicly accessible. All issues of such journals may be available for free, although sometimes only a limited number of issues are offered.

But despite the best efforts of your distance education provider, faculty, and librarians to make comprehensive information available to you online, there will be times when you need something in print format. If your online library is linked to a brick-and-mortar college or university, you will be able to borrow books and obtain copies of journal articles directly from the collection of print materials in that library. You can learn which books or journals are in the library through its online library catalog, available to you on your home computer 24 hours a day, seven days a week. You may even be able to fill out a form online to request that books or photocopies of journal articles be sent to your home. If not, there will be a telephone number for requesting materials.

Many online colleges or universities have access to a traditional library of print materials to supplement the online collection. If your online school has entered into a formal agreement with a traditional library where you can borrow books or request copies of articles, the books or articles can be sent directly to your home, at little or no cost to you. Usually, online institutions try to forge contracts with traditional libraries in areas close to where groups of their students live and work.

Once in a while you will be unable to locate books or articles through any of the channels already mentioned. Usually, a virtual library has a list of alternate means for getting materials, accompanied by information about the cost in time or money for the alternatives.

Here are some words of caution: Plan ahead! Traditional students who are on a campus that has a large library can pop into the building and check out a book or make photocopies without much forethought, but online learners must plan ahead. If what you need is not available online, you must give yourself several weeks to locate it and get it through other sources. Many of our students have had to compromise and settle for references of less relevance because they did not receive materials in time to meet the deadline for their papers. One student ran into that problem because a delivery service had left the photocopies at a garage several doors down the street, though she had specifically requested that the driver put them by *her* garage door. Even if materials are being sent directly from a school's traditional library, be prepared for unexpected and unavoidable delays and glitches.

With such a plethora of online resources and access to a library's print material, do you need anything else? Yes, there is more to an online library than electronic resources. Professional librarians who hold advanced degrees, working with the assistance of their trained staff, provide specialized services.

MORE PERSONAL ONLINE LIBRARY SERVICES

Even if you are a computer whiz or a confident user of electronic messaging, you may be surprised by how much a librarian's expertise can benefit your studies. One of the primary tasks of librarians is to provide guidance and instruction for searching the virtual library's online databases. Although finding what you need in the reserve collection or electronic journals may be an intuitive process that offers few challenges, there is quite a difference between *surfing* the Internet and *searching* databases effectively and efficiently. In fact, your surfing habits may even interfere with the development of good search skills. Some of our online students had to be "weaned" from surfing so they could learn the new processes required to access our university's databases and other electronic resources. We had to teach them a whole new set of tools.

If you are uncertain about where to begin your search for materials to use in your online course, ask your librarian to advise you. Usually the search will begin in one or more of the online databases, though librarians do not discount other information sources, including the World Wide Web. Experience has taught them how to delve into these other resources and to eliminate the chaff, retrieving only premium information.

Even the best online tutorials or guides may not answer your specific questions about how to use a particular database effectively and efficiently, but a one-to-one phone call or exchange of email messages with your librarian may be just the information you need. Online tutorials and guides usually cover only general searching techniques. Interacting with your librarian can introduce you to some elegant, efficient, and timesaving techniques over and above what is presented in instructional materials. So if you have followed the instructions for searching a database but still have not been able to pin down the materials or citations relevant to your class, let your librarian know where you've looked and the strategies you have used. He or she can analyze your technique and perhaps develop a different strategy that works. Like librarians at the reference desk of a bricks-and-mortar library, online librarians are used to finding the answers to a wide variety of questions. Sometimes it is as simple as the page numbers or the issue number of a journal article, or maybe the first name of the author of a book. Whatever the question, an online librarian won't give up until he or she has either found the answer or exhausted every possible channel. Not only will a librarian give you the answer, but he or she will also teach you how to find the information next time.

The online library provides several means by which students can get their study or research materials, whether in electronic or print format. However, once in a while you may need an esoteric book or journal article that seems not to be available anywhere or through any means. Don't be discouraged. Online librarians take delight in a seemingly hopeless quest—they don't give up until they are successful or have exhausted every possibility. As a self-directed learner and a competent professional in your field, you may be hesitant to ask your online librarian for assistance or guidance in these areas. It is a mistake not to ask for help. Too many students, especially those at the very beginning of their online experience, worry that asking questions will make them lose face. Don't hesitate to ask your online librarian questions. Don't worry about asking a "dumb question." The only dumb questions are those that should be asked but aren't.

As someone who returned to graduate school after more than twenty years, I know how intimidating the technological changes in libraries can be. Only the patient and nonjudgmental guidance of the university's librarians kept me from giving up the first semester. Like any librarians, online librarians are well aware of the challenges that face returning students, and are more than willing to help you overcome them.

WHAT TO LOOK FOR IN ONLINE LIBRARIES

Although your online college or university is responsible for providing your library services and resources, it is up to you to learn what a school's virtual library *really* has to offer. Start with the Web site for the online library. There should be a link to it from the school's home page, although it may not be called a "library" but something like "learning resource center."

If there is no readily visible link from the institution's home page, perhaps that is an indication that library support is a low priority and thus inadequate for your needs.

Look for information about and links to the various library resources mentioned above. If there is no toll-free number on the library's Web site, call the college or university and ask for contact information. If there are no real people in the online library or if you can't reach them easily, you should have second thoughts about whether that is the school you want to select.

As a summary, here is a checklist of the items mentioned in "Resources in the Online Library," the section that opened this chapter. A top-notch online library should provide all or most of these:

- Online citation/abstract or full-text databases
- A reserve collection
- Electronic journals
- Carefully selected links to Web sites
- Online tutorials and guides
- Home delivery of materials not readily available online
- Information about alternative ways to get materials

Don't hesitate to request more information about any of the resources, about databases, or about other pertinent matters of importance to you personally. In particular, be sure to ask how many publications are indexed in a database. What percentage of resources is full-text? Is your discipline well represented in the database? How far back do the books and articles go? Are there any extra fees? For example, how much does it cost to have a book or copy of a journal article delivered to your home? How long does delivery usually take?

In addition, you should also attempt to learn how the real people in the online library could assist you. Here is another checklist of the services that should be provided by online librarians:

- Suggesting where to start your search for information or materials
- Helping you develop good search strategies
- Assisting you in locating hard-to-find books or journals
- Identifying nearby libraries that you can use to supplement the virtual library
- Guiding you in evaluating resources

If the librarian appears unwilling to take the time to answer your questions now, or seems threatened by your questions, such an attitude should raise a red flag. Online librarians should be more than willing to respond to questions such as: How do you set up your online account? Are interlibrary loan services available? What reference services are available? When are they available? Are phone calls toll-free? Is there an online tutorial, guide, or orientation?

CONCLUSION

A complaint frequently made by my fellow online librarians is that their services and expertise are underused. Many online students do not take advantage of the various online resources provided by their schools. Instead, they spend hours searching the World Wide Web in vain hope of finding what they need for their courses. They have little inkling of their college or university's rich online resources, which have been specifically tailored to their needs and paid for by their tuition.

Don't shortchange yourself. Learn early in the game what your online library has to offer and make good use of it.

APPLICATION EXERCISE 15A

Evaluating Online Resources

In order to help you evaluate the quality and reliability of your online resources, ask the following questions:

- Who is the author and are his or her credentials recognized by other authorities in the discipline?

  ____

  ____

  ____

- With what institutions is the author or Web site affiliated and are those institutions accredited?

  ____

  ____

  ____

- Is the Web site connected with a governmental, educational, or commercial type of organization?

  ____

  ____

  ____

- How is the article documented and supported? What kind of evidence is used to support the article? Are statements and statistics cited and sources provided?

  _____

  _____

  _____

- Is the article written in a recognized style such as APA?

  _____

  _____

  _____

- How current is the author's work? How current are the citations?

  _____

  _____

  _____

■ ■ ■ ■ ■

CHAPTER 16

I HAVE MY ONLINE DEGREE— NOW WHAT DO I DO?

LESLIE BOWMAN

In this chapter, you will learn about:

- How the online degree is only the gateway to other opportunities
- Advice on how to look for places to use your learning online and offline

You now have your online degree, or you are about to finish. What do you do now? Whether you are looking for your first job or changing careers, searching for a job can seem like a daunting endeavor when you are first getting started. Although it is true that there are many things you can do to make the process go more smoothly, it does take a lot of planning, time, and effort. Even with a brand new online degree, jobs do not usually just fall into your lap, although that has been known to happen. Usually, when the perfect job does seem to just fall into your lap, it is as a result of your own efforts in job searching and networking.

There are no big secrets to job searching or to getting the job you want, but the skills and attitudes you have learned online will help. Above all else, your persistence to complete your online degree will make the biggest difference. Searching for a job is a numbers game that has a set procedure and requires persistence. The more contacts you make, the more chances that you will get a reply. You will also get more "no responses" or "no thank you responses" than you will get positive ones; that is just the way it always happens. Through your persistence, you will get positive responses that request more information and, hopefully, an interview that makes the entire process worthwhile.

Before you can even begin to think about finding and applying for jobs or networking, you have to be prepared to market the skills, experience, and talents you have identified and learned in your online program. By completing an online program, you have already demonstrated mastery of such skills as:

- Comparing, integrating, analyzing, and synthesizing information
- Coordinating information, tasks, and research
- Mentoring other online students in group projects and dealing with different personalities
- Negotiating ideas and assignments in online discussions and projects
- Adjusting schedules and timetables to complete online assignments

After you identify the skills you have acquired, you have to know what kind of job you want. You really need to target a specific job market, and then you research the companies that have job descriptions that interest you. Researching job descriptions does not mean looking for job vacancies and seeing what you need for that job. It means really investigating the inner workings of the company, and finding out if there are currently any jobs similar to what you want to do. Again, the information you have gained in your online program and the people you met should be of some assistance. Part of this process is identifying the specific course information and your online classmates who can be resources.

The point is, use your online knowledge, experience, and contacts.

After that, you can compare your skills and experience with the job description, and communicate with past online classmates to learn about job markets and descriptions. By doing this, you will get a pretty good idea about what kinds of jobs your online education and experience has prepared you for and what more, if anything, you need to do to compete in that job market. Knowing any limitations you may have can also help you prepare to overcome those limitations by concentrating on other strengths that are needed for a specific job.

If you are reading this information at the beginning of your online program, make sure you keep a record of people you meet online—what are their email addresses, locations, jobs, and areas of expertise? This information could become useful in the future.

Using your online skills and contacts, you should also research where the best job opportunities are in your field of interest. This is the time when you have to decide if and when you are willing to relocate. How long will you look in your current location without finding a job before you will consider moving? This is not a consideration to be taken lightly. Much will depend on your family situation. Include in your research any companies or possible jobs outside your current location. I looked for jobs all over the country even though I knew I would not consider moving. This gave me a pretty good idea of job locations, salaries, types of employers, job descriptions, and availability of jobs. Keep a list of companies as you do this research, and rank them according to how well they match your qualifications and skills.

Once you have evaluated your online experience and know what kinds of jobs are out there that really interest you and that you would really like to do, then it is time to begin preparing how you will demonstrate how well your qualifications meet those job requirements.

MARKETING YOUR ONLINE SKILLS AND TALENT

Most people have written a resume at some point either during college or their working years. You, again, have an edge because of all the writing a typical online program requires. But if you do not have a resume and are not sure how to write a professional resume, get a good resume book at your local library or bookstore. There are also Web sites that walk you through writing a professional resume. Your resume will change slightly with each job for which you apply, and you will want to keep copies of each resume you write because eventually you will use them more than once.

Increasingly, companies are using various online formats to process resumes. Your online experience again puts you at an advantage.

Along with a resume, you need to have a professional portfolio that demonstrates how your skills and experience have transferred into successful results. Professional or career portfolios are now being used by job seekers in other fields as well. A portfolio is a good way to expand upon the information in your resume, and demonstrate the skills and experience you gained in your online program far better than one piece of paper can do.

There are quite a few good Web resources and books about how to create a professional portfolio. It would be well worth your time to do a Web search and read some of the available information on how to put together an effective portfolio. Generally, there are several common sections in a portfolio that may include any of the following (but not necessarily all):

- Career summary and goals
- Resume
- Samples of your work
- Your marketable qualities, including online skills and experience
- Recommendation letters
- Conferences and presentations
- Awards and honors
- Professional organization memberships
- Volunteer work
- Transcripts, degrees
- Military records
- References

Remember that not everything listed is included in all portfolios. In some cases, you may have something of value to include that is not listed here. The primary elements are career summary and goals, marketable qualities, and samples of your work that demonstrate successful results. Volunteer work counts as experience, so don't forget to include that as well. While your resume focuses on a specific job target, the portfolio highlights everything you have accomplished in your online education and career.

In addition to print versions of your resume and portfolio, you should also have online versions of each. Your resume can easily be transferred to a single Web page. Your portfolio should be in a three-ring binder with a professional cover. You should also create a series of Web pages that correspond to the pages in your binder portfolio. There are some very good reasons for doing this and the single best example I can give you is my own personal experience.

I began the process six months before graduation, a strategy I highly recommend. I had a great resume and several job leads, but I received fewer responses than I would have liked. Eventually, I made a Web page and put all the information from my resume on my Web page. I also provided a link to a print copy of my resume. After that, when I wrote emails inquiring about employment, I included the URL for my Web page resume right in the body of the letter rather than attaching a file. And guess what? I started getting responses, far more responses than I had received with my resume as file attachments.

My online portfolio was a work in progress for many months; it still is and always will be. It started with a simple Web page on which I linked to projects I had done in graduate school that demonstrated my knowledge in specific skill areas. From there, the portfolio grew as I gained experience and completed other projects. You can and should start creating your portfolio while you are still in your online program. Add to it as you gain more and more experience in your online program, and your portfolio will be an outstanding representation of your career and educational accomplishments.

Beyond the professional resume and portfolio, there are some other ways in which you can prepare to market your skills and experience. You can and should join professional organizations in your field, and don't just join, but also become active in those organizations.

Volunteer for committee work and projects so that you meet people in the field and demonstrate both your willingness to work and your abilities. This will eventually become an important networking tool in your job search.

Write articles for trade magazines or business publications.

If you are currently working and looking at a future job change after obtaining your online degree, now is the perfect time to make use of the resources at your workplace. Apply the communication skills you have learned online. Volunteer to write the company newsletter or chair a committee. Offer to make key presentations at work. Keep copies of all professional writing. Take great care with your written online schoolwork, as this too can be an asset in your portfolio. All of this is concrete documentation of both your writing and communication skills, and your knowledge of your field.

Remember that everything you do, whether paid work, volunteer work, or college projects, counts as experience in your career field. It is important to document all of this experience in a career portfolio for later job searches.

FINDING JOB LEADS AND MAKING CONTACTS

Before you can begin to think about making contacts, you have to decide who to contact and why you will target that person or company in your job search efforts. This means that you have to determine your specific skills and interest, and also figure out what company will be interested in your skills and talent. As you start to list your skills, achievements, accomplishments, experience, and special talents, you also have to begin to think in terms of how these skills will benefit a future employer. Don't think of yourself in terms of a job title, either past, present, or future, but rather in terms of what you can do and how you can transfer your skills into new opportunities. This is also the time to polish your presentation skills and your business appearance. Remember that when you attend conferences or business organization meetings, the first impression that people get will be the lasting impression if and when you include these people in your network strategies.

By this time, hopefully, you have completed a professional online resume and career portfolio, and have begun attending conferences and professional organization meetings. You have volunteered to work on a committee and you are writing an article or two for publication in your field, or have completed outstanding online program papers and projects that are relevant to your career field. Through all these activities, you are already meeting and talking with people in your career field. But what are you saying to them and how is that helping or hurting your chances for prospective jobs?

An excellent strategy to help you when it comes to talking to people about yourself is to write and practice saying a one-minute "commercial" that tells who you are, your special talents, and your career goals. It is interesting to note that many people do not like to talk (or write) about themselves because they feel it is bragging. Women, especially, have a difficult time overcoming this barrier. On the other hand, as an online student, you probably have had to upload numerous biographical descriptions to various courses. You have this information—use it. The truth is that stating your qualifications and abilities is not bragging or boasting. It is simply stating facts, unless you are exaggerating and I strongly discourage that because it will come back to haunt you. If you do not tell prospective contacts and employers about yourself, then who exactly do you think will do that for you? No one will know if you do not tell him or her, and you cannot rely on your resume to do it alone. If you are talking by telephone, try to be comfortable talking about yourself. If you are emailing or writing an inquiry letter, then you should be comfortable writing about your accomplishments.

Employers want to know who you are and what you can do. And they will ask point blank in an interview, over the phone, or even in an email. Memorize your commercial and say it aloud enough times that it sounds natural. You can even use a shorter version at parties, presentations, conferences, and anywhere else you meet people. Remember that social contacts, including the people you met in your online program, can sometimes net very good employment contacts. Take some time, right this very minute, to sit down and write out a one-minute "commercial" about yourself. It might go something like this:

> Hi, my name is _____ and I just graduated from _____ with a _____ degree in _____ and I've been working full time as well at _____ Company. Working full time while attending online school has helped me develop outstanding time management skills through organization and prioritizing projects for both school and work. I don't have any trouble at all starting and completing projects and I enjoy working with people. I see these skills as being especially important in a _____ career.

Memorizing and practicing your commercial will make it sound natural and will also help you feel comfortable talking about yourself. Write a short version and once you have that down pat, practice editing it while speaking, because sometimes you may want to change the specifics depending on the person to whom you are talking.

When it comes to making contacts through phone calls, letters, and emails, people sometimes unknowingly sabotage their own efforts. There are several ways *not* to get a job, such as when you:

- Are not clear on what you really want to do
- Have not done your homework on jobs and companies
- Are too modest about promoting your skills and talents
- May not know how to market your skills and talents
- Are not really sure you want to make a change
- Are not sure how or where to find job leads
- Do not know how to effectively contact prospective employers
- Do not want to make cold calls
- Do not know how to network

So far, we have covered more than half of this list. Now it is time to tackle the real work of finding and landing a job you want, so it is time to cover the last four items on this list.

ONLINE JOB SEARCHING

Finding job leads online is a fairly simple process, although it may initially be time consuming. Before you begin, make sure you have assembled your resume and portfolio for copy/pasting, or attaching as a file, or typing in the information on the Web site. The process may be different for different search sites. When I first began job searching online, I went to all the better-known search sites and ran a quick search on jobs in my field. I was still in graduate school so I knew I was not ready to apply for any of those jobs, but I wanted to know which sites had the best track record for job listings in my field.

The major job search sites are:

- Monster.com (http://www.monster.com)
- Flipdog (http://www.flipdog.com)
- CareerBuilder (http://www.careerbuilder.com)
- HotJobs (http://www.hotjobs.com)

I would also suggest that you go to a good search engine (my recommendation is Google at http://www.google.com) and run a search for job search sites in your specific field to add to the list. A good key word combination is simply "_____ job listings." For example, you could try "marketing job listings" or "IT job listings." Once you have done that, then run a quick search on all the sites you have chosen to see how many job listings there are in your field. Bookmark all the sites that you will plan to use.

Next, go to each site, register, and complete the online resume format. After that, set up your automatic search agents on each site. I recommend using as many search agents as are available, each with slightly different key words. Personally, I used six search sites and five automatic search agents on each site. My resume was available on all the sites. Since I have many colleagues in the same field, I have left my search agents active so that when I get notification of a good job lead in an area where a colleague may have an interest, I send it along to that colleague. That is called networking and we will talk more about that later.

Basically, that is all there is to online job searching. It takes quite a bit of time initially to locate the right search sites and to get everything set up. But once that is done, it requires little time and effort to maintain as you get email notifications when jobs are listed that fit your search agents' criteria. I would like to mention that most of these sites also have user communities in which there are discussion forums, and sometimes chat rooms. I highly recommend visiting those and participating in some of the job search discussions. This is another way to network.

You never know when you may run into someone online in a discussion forum who knows someone who happens to work at a company that is looking for a person just like you.

When you receive notification of a job listing for which you would like to apply, then it is time to polish your cover letter and prepare to send it to the prospective employer. This is your initial employment inquiry and first impressions count for everything here. If you are unsure about writing a superb cover letter, there are many books and Web sites with instructions and examples for appropriate letters in different circumstances. My suggestion is to do your homework so that your letter stands out, gets the attention it deserves, and gets your foot in the door for a response and, hopefully, an interview.

This is where I must reiterate my recommendation to have an online resume so that you can include the URL in the body of the letter rather than attaching a file. I also strongly suggest that you include a comparison of your talents and skills with the employer's needs for the job listing. This type of letter explains in a concise manner exactly what you can do for the employer. The advantage is that it is short and simple, gets right to the bottom line, and does not take more than a minute to read. This type of letter is also different from the usual letters that are received and, as a result, it immediately piques the reader's interest and curiosity, which maintains interest long enough to quickly click on the resume URL to find out more about you. Believe me when I tell you that this works! And it works far more often than a resume file attached to an email letter.

THE DREADED COLD CALL

I dislike cold calls as much as the next person does, but in job searching they are a necessity. Two-thirds of jobs are never advertised. This is called the "hidden job market" and you need to understand how to work this job market. In some cases, jobs may not even exist when you write to inquire about an employment position. In those cases, you are writing to propose a job that you can do that will benefit the company. In essence, you are creating a job for yourself and proposing it to various prospective employers. Even though you have search agents set up and you are pouring over the classified ads both locally and online, you need to set aside at least half of your search time and effort to focus on the hidden job market. You should think about how you could become a company's solution to a problem or a challenge. Always think in terms of what you can do for a company that no one else can do, and how it will benefit the company to hire you for a job that you propose doing for them.

If you are just starting out in a field or are changing careers, you may not have a lot of experience with which to negotiate an employment position. In situations like these, you may have to take temporary or short-term jobs to gain the experience you need. In some cases, you might even offer to work on a contract basis with permanent employment pending upon successful completion of a project. There are quite a few job seekers that have earned permanent employment with companies by sticking their necks out and saying, "I can do _____ for you better than anyone else and I am willing to work on a temporary trial basis to prove my competence and experience for this job."

The bottom line is that cold calling shows initiative and self-confidence, skills and attitudes you gained in your online education. Cold calling demonstrates that you are assertive and proactive, which are qualities that employers look for in the people they hire. In some cases, employers are so impressed with the sheer "gutsiness," that they find it difficult to say no to an interview. This is, again, a situation of being different, and that means getting attention and piquing curiosity so that an employer wants to know more about you and what you can do.

Cold calls can be done by phone and by email. The key is to keep the "pitch" short and to the point. On the phone, simply say, "Hi, my name is _____ and I have _____ years of experience as _____ specializing in _____. I have a degree in _____ from _____ and I recently completed _____ (state project and results). When can I come in for an interview?"

If you use email, you say a little more, but not much. I have sent numerous "cold call" emails to prospective employers. The reason I use email is that I work online and all of my work is for employers who are geographically distant. I have followed the same procedure for some time now with better than average success. Here is what I do to propose a "job" with an employer that has no job listings:

- Research the company and the department for which my experience has prepared me to work
- Identify "holes" in employment areas that I can fill
- Make a chart of my qualifications and employer's needs (based on my research)
- Write a short email, including the URL for my CV and my career portfolio

In my emails, I include only three short paragraphs:

1. A one-sentence description of my purpose in writing followed by a description of specific qualifications that are best suited for this particular company (these will change in each letter).
2. A description of a successful project and an explanation of how I can do the same for this employer. Keep in mind that at this point I have researched to determine that this employer currently does *not* have someone doing what I am proposing to do.

3. The basic thank you, with an invitation to visit my career portfolio Web site and view my online CV (URLs are included here) and a request for a convenient time to discuss my proposal.

That's all. Short, sweet, and simple. Why does this work? It works for all the reasons listed throughout this chapter. It is different—it shows initiative, assertiveness, and self-confidence. It gets attention and piques interest, and the employer will want to know more about this person who has the guts to say or write, "Here is what I can do for you; when would be the best time for us to talk?"

NETWORKING IN PERSON AND ONLINE

Networking is simply using friends, family, and acquaintances—including those you have learned with online—to locate employment opportunities. Contrary to what some people believe, this does not mean begging for a job. Many of the best networking contacts are found quite by accident. You may be at a get-together and find yourself talking to someone about your job search. As the conversation continues, he or she suddenly says, "You know, my cousin knows a guy whose father-in-law works at XYZ Company and he was talking the other day about looking for someone who could do what you do. If you're interested, I could give him a call." You might even come across these kinds of comments in your online courses. This type of contact happens more than you might think.

If you're just starting your online education, look for networking contacts.

It happens at social events, online courses, business organization meetings, and even casual conversation in the grocery store or day-care center. The important thing to remember is not to be embarrassed by the fact that you do not have a job. The more you talk about your job search, the more the chances are that someone will know someone else who could be a very good contact for you.

One of the best ways to network, other than friends and family, is online. By running a simple search, you can locate several online communities in your field of interest. Many of these have discussion forums, and it is a very good idea to participate in those forums. Just as you would attend conferences and business organization meetings in person, you can also attend online discussions and meetings. The contacts you make online will be every bit as valuable as the ones you make in person. I belong to three online communities in my career field and I have met several contacts who have, in turn, put me in touch with other contacts, which led to lucrative work contracts.

This seems an appropriate time and place to mention references. Choose your references carefully. Recently I sent a "cold call" inquiry letter that netted a response requesting that I fill out the attached paperwork for employment while my references were being contacted (they were listed on my CV web page). To make a long story short, of my four references, only one responded to the request by this prospective employer. One was seriously ill, another had left the country for a job overseas, and another was just too busy. I discovered this after trying to contact each of them myself. I had to scramble to arrange for three further references in a two-day period of time, and it was a trifle embarrassing to have to explain to a prospective employer why three of my references could not respond with letters. Suffice it to say, I got the job and I owe those three people in a big way for those wonderful letters they wrote on such short notice.

Again, choose your references carefully and keep in touch with them, including any possible references you've met in your online courses. My mistake was that I had lost touch with two of my references and another was ill, unbeknownst to me. My suggestion would be to maintain regular contact with your references after initially receiving permission to list them as references. Each time you get a serious prospect that indicates a call to your references, contact those people to let them know to expect a call (or email as the case might be). This might very well prevent some headaches down the road for you. Keep in mind also that your references will change as you gain experience in your career. It is always best to use recent references as opposed to ones from several years ago.

CONCLUSION

There is an old saying that goes something like this: "It's all in who you know." In today's online world, this is far more accurate than many people realize. I know that it has been true for me. The colleagues in my network look out for one another. If I run across a job that I know would suit a particular colleague, I send it right away. Likewise, colleagues have sent me potential employment opportunities as well. This type of network does not happen overnight, but rather one person at a time, over a period of time. My networking began when I was still in school, and has continued to grow as I have met new people in my field through online classes and online communities.

Keep in touch with your online classmates after you have graduated and make a pact to help each other out in the job search.

One strategy that has worked well for my colleagues and me is to set up a "club" on Yahoo.com through which we keep in contact via email messages. When any of us runs across a job prospect in which others may be interested, we send it out in a group email message. I have found several good contacts that way.

Networking and cold calling are valuable strategies for locating good jobs. These are also the strategies that take the most time and effort to maintain. Remember that your time and effort will be repaid many times over throughout your working lifetime. Most working adults change careers an average of seven times during their working years. Your online skills, networking, and your ability to market your talents will be your best advantage for many years to come. Best wishes for a successful career search, now and in the future.

Creating a Career Action Plan

A Career Action Plan is a road map that takes you from choosing an occupation to becoming employed in that occupation to reaching your long-term career goals. In order to help you develop a career action plan, respond to the following questions:

1. Employment History (List your jobs from most to least recent.)

NAME/LOCATION OF EMPLOYER	TITLE	DATES

2. Education and Training (Beginning with high school, list the schools you have attended, their locations, dates attended, and degrees earned.)

SCHOOL	LOCATION	DATES ATTENDED	DEGREES

3. Additional Training

_____

_____

_____

4. Professional Licenses

_____

_____

5. Volunteer and Other Unpaid Experience (Activities and Responsibilities)

_____

_____

_____

_____

_____

_____

6. Self-Assessment Results (Tools such as the Myers-Briggs Type Indicator are described at such Web sites as careerplanning.about.com.)

NAME OF TOOL:

_____

_____

NAME OF TOOL:

_____

_____

The following occupations were indicated as occupations that might be suitable based on the results of the self-assessment:

_____

_____

_____

_____

7. Short-Term Career Plan (one month to one year)

Occupational Goals: Within the next year, what would you like to accomplish with your career?

_____

_____

_____

_____

8. Long-Term Career Plan (one year to five years)

Occupational Goals: Within the next five years, what would you like to accomplish with your career?

_____

_____

_____

_____

BOOK RECOMMENDATIONS

Baber, A., & Waymon, L. (1995). *How to fireproof your career: Survival strategies for volatile times.* New York: Berkley Publishing Group.

Baber, A., & Waymon, L. (2001). *Make your contacts count: Networking know-how for cash, clients, and career success.* New York: AMACOM.

Bernstein, A. B., & Schaffzin, N. R. (2000). *The Princeton review guide to your career.* New York: Random House.

Bolles, R. N. (2003). *What color is your parachute?* Berkeley, CA: Ten-Speed Press.

Covey, S. R. (1990). *The seven habits of highly effective people.* New York: Simon & Schuster.

Fein, R. (2000). *101 dynamite questions to ask at your job interview.* Manassas Park, VA: Impact Publications.

Gurney, D. W (2000). *Headhunters revealed.* Los Angeles: Hunter Arts Publishing.

Herman, R., Olivo, T., & Gioia, J. (2002). *Impending crisis: Too many jobs, too few people.* Winchester, VA: Oakhill Press.

Johnson, S., (1998). *Who moved my cheese?* New York: Putnam Publishing Group.

Mesiti, P. (1998). *Wake up and dream.* Author.

Mesiti, P. (1994). *Dreamers never sleep.* Author.

Ryan, R. (2000). *60 Seconds and you're hired.* New York: Penguin.

EPILOGUE

KEN W. WHITE, TINA MARIE NIES,
AND JASON D. BAKER

In this epilogue, you will learn about:

- Online education and ethical behavior
- Wisdom from graduating online students
- The value of lifelong learning

When it came to writing an epilogue for this handbook, the major question concerned what themes of the book we would like to leave you with. For example, an obvious theme is the need for the online student to take responsibility for his or her own learning. But that one has been emphasized thoroughly by our contributors. We decided to close with a three-fold charge for prospective online learners: (1) a call to ethical education, (2) a call to heed the wisdom of those learners who have gone before you, and (3) a call to embrace learning as a lifelong activity.

ETHICS IN THE ONLINE CLASSROOM

The online classroom cannot flourish unless both instructors and students use it according to a standard of fair conduct. In other words, "ethics" is a necessary consideration for any effective participation in an online learning environment.

Ethics refers to a code of conduct based on standards that everyone in a collective group can agree on, whether that group is a nation, a culture, or an online classroom. Codes of ethics are derived from the beliefs, values, expectations, and needs of a group—its history, traditions, principles, and common sense about acceptable behavior. The history of philosophical thoughts shows that honesty and justice are major values that help to promote cooperation in many groups. These values are also beneficial for the success of an online classroom.

You choose online education expecting that you will get truthful information, share real ideas with other students, be able to ask authentic questions, and generally engage in open learning transactions. All of these expectations relate to the general expectation about communication in an educational setting, an expectation we might label as the need for an "ideal learning situation." Authentic education—online or traditional—depends on students believing in the honesty and fairness of others in order to learn something to enhance their personal and professional lives. Although they may not have this expectation in their personal and professional lives, they recognize the need for a "clearing" in education where ideas can be shared and challenged without the distortions of such factors as politics. They understand that human prejudices exist in all human situations, but they also understand that the special qualities of a classroom encourage those prejudices to be openly discussed.

Although all human relationships require some level of trust, relationships among students in an online classroom are based on trust. Without the typical information of face-to-face situations where facial gestures and body language tell us whether to trust someone or not, when an online student states an opinion or fact, other online students must trust that the person is telling the truth and not trying to deceive or manipulate. If this trust is violated, and online students begin to doubt that they can trust one another or the instructor, the online classroom can become so severely constrained that authentic learning may become impossible. Cooperation can end and the online class reduced to fulfilling a series of meaningless technicalities.

A COVENANTAL APPROACH
TO ONLINE EDUCATION

In the online classroom, where you cannot see the other student and have no personal history, standards of ethical behavior are crucial. The trust of online students will be increased by the knowledge that the classroom holds to certain ethical standards. Ethical behavior may not come naturally to you, the instructor, and other students in the class, so it is necessary to develop a set of principles for participating in the online learning environment. We recommend that online instructors and learners consider developing a covenant to provide an ethical framework to support and enhance their online learning endeavor.

In the early Near East, covenants were used for a variety of agreements from business loans to international treaties. Today, some schools use covenants to state the principles of teaching and learning that guide the activities in their classrooms. Unlike mission and vision statements, a classroom covenant is an agreed-upon declaration of teaching and learning practices that inform and monitor the educational experience. Such a covenant is detailed, practical, and observable. It is not a one-way declaration by instructors or a wish list by students; rather, the covenant is a mutual agreement among teachers and students in which they pledge to conduct themselves according to a set of standards. We offer the following components as a starting point for the development of such a document. First, to ensure that the faculty member exhibits sound ethical behavior, you should expect the following standards in your online class. The online instructor should:

- Prepare diligently to teach the online course
- Clearly articulate the tasks and responsibilities of the instructor and students
- Make course content available in a timely manner
- Deal consistently and fairly with all students
- Maintain confidentiality of student information
- Discuss ethical standards expected for the particular course and curriculum
- Follow copyright and intellectual property laws
- Always exhibit the principles he or she purports to stand for

In addition, online learners have their covenant requirements. To ensure that you exhibit sound ethical behavior, other online students should expect that you show certain attitudes and follow certain standards. You should:

- Interact with your instructor and classmates by computer and develop a partnership with the instructor and students at a distance
- Dedicate at least the same amount of time and effort to an online course that you would to a traditional course
- Show self-discipline to learn without face-to-face interaction with your instructor and other students
- Show the time-management skills that enable you to balance online course work with your professional and personal responsibilities
- Meet due dates and keep track of your assignments when using the online course format
- Show an appreciation of and commitment to the convenience and flexibility that online courses provide
- Learn to use the technology necessary to complete course work
- Treat your instructor and fellow classmates with respect at all times

Although you're welcome to adopt these sixteen points as written, ideally a class covenant would be developed at the beginning of an online course as a joint effort between the instructor and learners, with provisions for dealing with those actions that violate specific terms of the covenant. All parties would then electronically sign the covenant and use the effort as the starting point for a rich online learning experience.

SUGGESTIONS FROM ONLINE STUDENTS

Despite all of the preliminary labor that instructors and students can put into a course, such as course preparation and the development of a class covenant, there is no guarantee that the result will be an effective learning experience for everyone involved. Throughout this book you have read numerous chapters providing guidance on various topics, from tips for effective online communication to how to use a virtual library, all of which can help you prepare to succeed in the online environment. However, there's also value in getting some real world tips from those students who have gone before you. Just as many of us would scope out professors and courses, to get the "real story" before registering, we thought it would be useful to offer some candid suggestions from online learners. We asked a group of students what advice they would give to someone starting an online program. We've grouped their responses into three areas—workload, people, and personal—and trust that you'll glean some practical guidance as you prepare to take the plunge.

Workload

- Don't let the workload scare you. After a couple of classes you will naturally become more adept at organizing your time. Don't worry that the family won't survive a few hours without you or feel guilty about laying more work on them. What you are doing will benefit them as well and they too will naturally adapt after a few classes.

- Don't enter this program thinking that because it's online it will be easier. Make sure you are confident in yourself and your ideas and let the university tone your ability to reflect this confidence in the online environment. And make sure to pay attention—you are as much a teacher to yourself and others as the assigned instructor is to you!

- Be patient and give it about three courses to begin to feel comfortable and adjust. Learn an organizing technique to work school into your routine, I believe that you can't find a better way to receive an education. Online education is the best value for my money, allowing me to obtain my degree under four years and not have to go to school like my friends do. And finally, don't give up. Time flies so in an accelerated online program, with a new course every five weeks, it is amazing how quickly your degree can be completed.

■ Take a time management course, a speed reading class, get a backup computer (preferably a laptop), say good-bye to your family and friends, figure on gaining weight and getting little sleep, and get ready for the ride of your life.

■ Time management is necessary to fit all the assignments, like all the reading and writing we must do, and it will teach us not to procrastinate and put things off until the last minute. Speed reading helps and will give you more time with your family and friends.

■ Once enrolled, you have to remain motivated while keeping your goal in mind. I think the best motivator when I began was making a schedule of my entire curriculum and placing it in the area of our house where I did my homework. After completing each course I would mark the course out with a line and have a little celebration. That way I could remain focused on my goal and see my past accomplishments. It's difficult to remain motivated if you don't know where the finish line is.

■ Develop a devoted sense of discipline. Taking classes online is convenient but that doesn't mean it's easier. You really have to be committed to your goal because you could easily "blow off" homework or discussion time. It's easy to say, "I don't think I will log on tonight," when you know you should. It's too easy to get behind that way. I would also invest in a laptop. I can safely say that I spent 30 percent of my class away from home—business trips, camping trips, family outings, and so on. I would have never been able to do it if I hadn't had my laptop.

■ Don't even think about starting a program like this unless you are ready to commit a minimum of 20–25 hours a week to doing homework and writing papers. You must be dedicated to finish what you start while maintaining your normal everyday duties at home and at work.

■ Start off organized. You have to get into a routine for this to work well, so decide what time is going to be spent on school and stick to it (it will vary some depending on the workload for each class). Also, try to retain as much information as you can because it's all good information. I would also recommend keeping the books from the classes that you most enjoyed, or those that apply to your job. That is one thing I wish I had done.

People

■ Instructors are human too. If something unusual comes up, talk to them and work out a solution that is acceptable to both of you. If you don't understand what is expected—ask.

■ The eTeacher is a different breed, just like the successful eLearner. He or she has to be up to the task, adapt with the class, not be fearful of new technologies, and willing to seek training in this process of eTeaching just as he or she sought training in his or her area of expertise.

- From my experience of being an online learner for four years, I think establishing community is one of the most important things the instructor can do to facilitate learning. The instructor begins with the end in mind by stating the desired outcomes at the beginning of the class. The successful online instructor empowers the students for a mutual learning experience that gets every student involved with his or her own education.

- When a group assignment seems to become a one-person event, sometimes a phone call is more effective than an email. Talk to each other. There is almost always an explanation and a hurdle that can be overcome—*almost* always.

- You must get into the group discussions to take advantage of the online learning environment. The classes that I learned the most in are the classes in which I got heavily involved in the classroom discussions. Some of the best discussions came when the instructor got heavily involved in the classroom and asked some probing questions. It would really be nice to be able to have the instructors graded on this and then be able to select the instructors who really want to teach the students.

- The eLearner has to respond to the discussion boards—be willing to take the risk to post their responses. They have to be willing to engage the class in discussion, taking the time to write out answers in a thoughtful and complete but concise manner.

- You have to be willing to work hard—eLearners have a tough job to do. Not only do they have to respond to the teacher's discussion items and prepare the assignments, but they have to read each and every posting. After all, this is the stuff that eClassroom discussions are made of. Without that exchange, substantial learning is lost.

Personal

- You still do not have the time you had before school and I can't count the number of times I had to tell my kids I couldn't because I had school work to do, but this gets better as time management improves!

- I have gained 25 pounds in the last $2\frac{1}{2}$ years; I know this is a feeble excuse but I usually played a lot of racquetball and softball, but since I started school those were a casualty. Plus, when you are up late doing school work the call of ice cream gets louder! Did I mention "up late doing school work" in the previous sentence? Well, this is an understatement, I have averaged 5 hours' sleep a night during a school week. Then on my first day off I sleep until my body tells me to get up. There have been many nights of falling asleep at the keyboard and waking up with a very sore neck!

- When you get a holiday break, take it. The little you will gain from reading ahead or trying to do assignments ahead of time will not be worth what you will lose in R&R and face time with family and friends.

- An important step you should take even before enrolling is to talk with your family and make sure they are willing to sacrifice all the hours it will take in homework and studying. Without their blessing it would be virtually impossible to remain focused, get the education you are paying for, and/or even finish the program.

- After you decide what you really want, you need to involve family, friends, and management staff at work. Everyone who gets a piece of your time and is involved in your life must know the commitment you are about to sign up to and what is going to be expected to complete this program. It's not an easy thing to do when you have to tell your son that you can't take him to a ball game because you have to write a paper for school. I can't tell you how many times my wife has wanted to go on vacation and I told her that I had a group assignment and presentation due that week and I would not be able to go. These scenarios need to be communicated and the person must be able to accept those types of sacrifices in order to complete this type of program. But once you finish, you will feel like you can accomplish anything.

- You will have the most exciting, challenging experience of your life. The program is very rewarding but it takes a very serious, dedicated person to follow through on the individual and learning assignments. You must know how to manage your time for school and fit your lifestyle around study time. Make sure you have the support of family and friends to help in those times you can't be there to attend the kid's sports practice and family get together because you have research and papers to write. But the feeling you have after completing the courses for your degree is one of knowledge, growth, maturity, and accomplishment that is impossible to describe.

- I have been an online learner now for four years. By putting more time and effort into this type of education, I feel like I have received much more. I have established virtual friendships all over the world. I have developed more self-discipline in all the other areas of my life and I have become an independent learner.

- Get ready for a fun-filled roller coaster ride of knowledge. You will meet many people from all parts of the country, even some from overseas. The classes will be hard, but if it was easy everyone would have a degree and it would be worthless. When you are ready to quit, dig deep for that extra push, and if it doesn't work take a short break—this really worked for me. If I can do it, you can do it!

BECOMING A LIFELONG LEARNER

We are learners by nature. When we are born, we begin using all of our senses to learn about the world. We hear our parents speak to us and learn to recognize that we are not alone. When we are alone and scared, we feel their touch and learn what makes us feel warm and secure. We see their loving faces and look around at the wonders that will later become so familiar that we give them little thought and take them for granted. To youngsters, learning is exciting; in fact, we don't always think of it as learning—we are just having fun. We explore, experiment—often to the chagrin of our parents—we play, we imagine, we want to know everything. Then in our teen years, we begin to think we know it all—our parents can't possibly know better than we do whether the lawn mower will break if we run it down the rocky alley with the blades running. And in our late 20s we finally start to see that we really have lots more in life to learn, and as each year passes, we begin to realize how little we knew back when we thought we knew it all.

Of course learning is not done only in school—we learn through our everyday experiences. Becoming an involved, active person is what active lifelong learning is all about. Many of us deliberately plan our learning by going to college and graduate school, staying up to date in our career fields, taking enrichment classes, reading how-to books, and more. Others take a more passive approach to learning, and only plan to learn what they must.

Learning stimulates the brain and keeps our minds functioning at optimal levels. Even when we don't think we are learning, we are. We learn from life experiences, formal education, work-related activities, and family interactions. Every day we have the potential to learn, even without becoming an active learner. We meet people, hear their stories, and watch TV, where we might learn to slipcover a chair or what an aardvark eats with its long snout. We have the potential to learn through our good and our bad days. We have the opportunity to learn every day of our lives, and most of us do. It doesn't have to be planned, but it's always experienced.

As you have read in this book, online learning is also an important tool in lifelong learning. Because of our new technology and busy lifestyles, the online environment has made learning easy to fit into any schedule. Society is finally encouraging active lifelong learning—in large part because of significant workplace and technological changes. Active lifelong learning requires us to take an active role and recognize that we continue to learn every day of our lives. We must learn from every experience we have, and change our attitude about learning, thinking, and our abilities. Instead of passively learning as we all do, we take action. We create the experiences we want to learn from by taking classes, reading books and magazines, visiting museums, surfing the Internet, and more. As busy adults we want relevant, valuable, familiar, goal-oriented, practical, and useful learning experiences. We do not appreciate wastes of time or money. We want to feel respect and to be encouraged to share our experience and knowledge. What we need to do for ourselves is enhance our motivation and decrease our barriers. That is our responsibility as active lifelong learners.

Some challenges to active lifelong learning include the fact that many adults assume they can't learn. They believe that they've been in the same position for so long that it's too hard or too late to learn anything new. It can be hard at first to enter a structured learning environment after a long absence, but it's not impossible. We just have to retrain our brain to think as we did when we were young and bring back those critical thinking and problem-solving skills that worked so well when we were 10 and plotted to take over the neighborhood fort.

Here are a few simple steps that you can take to help tune your mind toward a deliberate pattern of lifelong learning:

- Start a journal and make regular entries
- Identify your personal interests
- Look at both your current work situation and your goals; identify areas for learning and growth
- Decide what type of learning fits you best
- Search the Internet for learning opportunities
- Find at least one volunteer opportunity that fits your schedule and interests
- Determine (and find) what formal learning options you need or want to meet your goals and interests

It is never too late to become a proactive lifelong learner, and online education gives you an opportunity.

CONCLUSION

The ideal conclusion for this book is for you, the reader, to rush off and take an online course that proves to be a rich educational experience beyond your wildest dreams. If you've already had some experience with online learning, perhaps this book has equipped you with the knowledge and insight to improve your abilities as an online learner. Regardless of your experience with online learning, we trust that this book has shed some light on the many opportunities available and the best way to take advantage of them. Our hope is that such opportunities don't simply create a population of better-educated people, but better people.

INDEX